Body Language

Use Non-verbal Communication And Nlp
To Influence And Persuade People

*(Learn Techniques That Psychologists And Fbi
Agents Use To Read People)*

Harvey Furnham

Published By **Oliver Leish**

Harvey Furnham

All Rights Reserved

Body Language: Use Non-verbal Communication And Nlp To Influence And Persuade People (Learn Techniques That Psychologists And Fbi Agents Use To Read People)

ISBN 978-1-77485-523-2

No part of this guidebook shall be reproduced in any form without permission in writing from the publisher except in the case of brief quotations embodied in critical articles or reviews.

Legal & Disclaimer

The information contained in this ebook is not designed to replace or take the place of any form of medicine or professional medical advice. The information in this ebook has been provided for educational & entertainment purposes only.

The information contained in this book has been compiled from sources deemed reliable, and it is accurate to the best of the Author's knowledge; however, the Author cannot guarantee its accuracy and validity and cannot be held liable for any errors or omissions. Changes are periodically made to this book. You must consult your doctor or get professional medical advice before using any of the suggested remedies, techniques, or information in this book.

Upon using the information contained in this book, you agree to hold harmless the Author from and against any damages, costs, and expenses, including any legal fees potentially resulting from the application of any of the information provided by this guide. This disclaimer applies to any damages or Injury caused by the use and application, whether directly or indirectly, of any advice or information presented, whether for breach of contract, tort, negligence, personal injury, criminal intent, or under any other cause of action.

You agree to accept all risks of using the information presented inside this book. You need to consult a professional medical practitioner in order to ensure you are both able and healthy enough to participate in this program.

Table Of Contents

Chapter 1: Body Language In Relationships 1

Chapter 2: Psychological Manipulation Techniques.. 3

Chapter 3: Cues That Say It All Context Overrides Words 22

Chapter 4: Various Methods Of Connecting 47

Chapter 5: How To Read And Recognize Emotions... 67

Chapter 6: All About Mirroring............... 85

Chapter 7: Nonverbal Socializing............ 99

Chapter 8: Expressions Of The Face 104

Chapter 9: How The Legs Show What The Minds Wants To Do 106

Chapter 10: Power Of Hands Power Of Hands... 112

Chapter 11: The Secret Handshake 119

Chapter 12: Touch................................ 129

Chapter 13: Unknown Ingredient In Body Language 137

Chapter 14: Body Langue In The Area Of Work 143

Chapter 15: Social Body Language Through Body Contact Touching 150

Chapter 16: Picking Up On Deceptive Body Language Behavioral Clusters 157

Chapter 17: Don't Forget To Join It! 162

Chapter 18: Speed-Reading People 168

Chapter 19: Body Language In Negotiation 179

Chapter 1: Body Language In Relationships

It is standard to utilize body language when seeking someone to date, especially at the context of a party that is loud. Learn about the things that will give you positive or negative impressions while looking for an ideal date.

Move your body in the direction of the person. This is the most effective way to demonstrate that you're curious. Take a look at the person in the eyes, then turn your gaze down before looking at them again. Slowly, as if you were trying to study the person.

Do not lean forward and put your feet in a cross. The position of the scissors in a standing position is unattractive because it demonstrates an insecurity and lack of confidence.

Do not rest your hands or place both hands into your pockets.

Do not get too close to someone until you are able to sense an interest. What can you tell whether you are being viewed as attractive by someone? Take a look at the following article to get an idea of body language to look out for in order to determine if they are attracted to you.

The person is looking at you, and their eyes raise.

Try to stand or sit in a better position can be a sign that someone is trying to create an impression.

Being able to touch oneself wherever one is with the help of combing one's hair with hands or putting on clothing while looking at someone else shows curiosity.

The speed at which you lift your shoulders shows the person believes in good motives and eager to get to meet you.

What you've discovered about eye contact micro-expressions and the positions of feet and hands can be utilized when you are dating. Be confident, as your feelings are likely to be evident through your body language too.

Chapter 2: Psychological Manipulation Techniques

You've heard of manipulating others through social media or how you can make use of it and how it can be most likely to be used to make you perform tasks that others want them to complete. Whatever the case, learning about the techniques of manipulating your mind is helpful to develop your defense strategies or apply them in secret on others (on their positive outcomes naturally).

Usually, putting someone else down is not a good idea. If you put another person down verbally is a risk. the possibility of appearing as personal attacks.

This can cause them to scream and they will not portray you in a positive image. It's not a good idea to attempt to persuade them to do something you would like to do.

However, the hurdles are lowered through laughter. The truth is that jokes are fun and generally not offensive, except for certain alternative comics.

It'll work in the same way if you decide to make

your anger the form of a joke, however it won't leave visible marks.

A good way to do this is to place your joke into the third person "Other people" ...," this kind of thing. If the other person believes that the joke is directed at them, you can disqualify the person with a snarky line such as "except for the current company Of course."

The Internet is constantly doing this. Therefore, make announcements. A carefully selected group of cats were the eight out of 10 cats with owners who preferred one particular brand. They got the result they sought by limit the sample size to a minimum and by carefully crafting the question in an approach that even an elected official would be jealous.

The majority of people will not question "fact" statements , mainly when you're only using them sparingly and proving them by citing some kind of "a survey I've seen or read about ..."

If you doubt factual information, that's better since those seeds are planted into the brain of the other person. Much like the moon landings, most of the world wonders whether they actually happened. If they did, I believe that a spacecraft did indeed arrive as you can see but I'm not sure who was on it or if they survived radiation and other dangers-the seeds of doubt are being planted. If it was that easy back in the 1960s, why haven't we returned with all of the technological advances. It's not even to compete with and the Russians and the Chinese. But, yeah, I'm digressing.

It's true that a majority of the time, moon landings don't worry the majority of us. But , we can utilize other supposedly reliable facts to convince others of our views and, surprisingly, control their thinking.

To accomplish it, one doesn't need the appearance of David Copperfield or Criss Angel. We've been practicing the "impossible" techniques for months and weeks.

Instead, you can create a variety of evidence to assist you in proving the things you're trying to alter.

Street fraudsters are using patsys as well as stooges. It's lots of effort and the support of others.

In the minds of other people creating the seeds of thought works wonderfully to induce hallucinations. Give them a few weeks or days and they'll be able to do almost all the manipulating. Then they create their unique idea, and that's what you originally desired. Result!

Wellness and Psychology

Healthful living services are marketed worldwide as a solution to preventive medicine that can lead to good health and long life spans. Wellness isn't just for people who have already been sick, but for those who are looking to remain healthy. In this article we will look at the notion of wellbeing in the perspective of mental well-being in which psychology and wellness are able to work together to offer the best psychological foundation for happiness and stability over the long term.

Introduction: What exactly is per-sae well-being? It's the absence of sickness and a feeling of well-being. It's not intended for those who have symptoms of illness, and are candidates for care. When you go to a wellness exam, which involves the patient going through a variety test of their physical condition, they're qualified to participate in an exercise program when they are able to can pass the test the tests and have a healthy. If they are not in a state of health that is good at any point it is considered a condition that requires treatment because they will require treatment for a condition which has been discovered even though it was not evident prior to the test.

Health plans are based by assuming that adjustments in lifestyle and preventive measures could prevent or minimize the risk of developing health problems in the future. This is particularly evident in Genetic tests, which are used to determine the presence of defective genes (genes with a fault in transmitting or repressing functions in the near future). This could mean that you could be at risk of certain diseases such as cancer or other problems in the near future. But, these are based on statistical probability and are not a final forecast. So, from a wellness perspective and based on their current state of performance, it is possible for the individual to alter their behavior patterns to an alternative that is healthier. To quit smoking for instance you should exercise more often and consume a vegetarian diet. It may sound strange to try even though there aren't any signs however the fact that the results of a Blood test suggests a future health issue could be the trigger for progress regardless of the fact that the gene does not express it's predictive. It is possible that you are at the highest chance of getting one particular kind of skin cancer, for example that you are in a western-style sunless area in Scandinavia and it's extremely unlikely that your exposure to the Sun can cause cancer to spread unlike living in Australia where exposure to the Sun is more prevalent but in reality it is skin cancer that is the most fatal cause of death in Australia. You also have a option to choose how you live, as long as you can live a healthy health!

What exactly is wellness? It's the absence of sickness and a feeling of well-being 1. The wellness program is created to offer healthy people who wish to remain in good health with guidance and medical care. The goal, of course is that the money you put into good health habits today will enable for a longer and healthy life, and decrease the risk of developing serious illnesses. There is a chance of getting unintentionally sick without having a health component in your planning and the price of time, resources as well as disruptions to your family and work can be devastating. Health and wellness is a priority reserved for those who are wealthy enough to pay for studies of top quality in their current condition of health and benefit from long-term prevention of disease. The human body functions more efficiently and for longer time than any machine that has been tuned to perfection that is well-maintained and not neglected. This is particularly true for employees who have to be aware of their health in order in order to perform each day for the benefit of their company. Health issues can be detrimental to the business they manage in the short-term. For instance In China businesses, the majority of owners are in charge of the business, regardless of how small or large They are in every decision, and every person below them is content. We can become extremely emotional and depressed when events go wrong, and blame everyone but ourselves for our difficulties. If they are suffering from a permanent disability, their business will be impacted because of managers and employees having no ability to make decision about their condition. The business will be wise to remain stagnant until the owner is back to healthy. So, the Chinese businessman who frequently chain smokes drinks a lot of alcohol, and eats a lot is a good person to make a change in their lifestyle and remain in control of the business. The most obvious solution is, naturally, to be to stop micromanaging and develop into more effective in leading other people.

Therapy and Psychological Health has been well ahead of curve in terms of health for many years to a certain extent. Through offering corporate training in the areas that deal with stress, managerial consulting and mental health, EAP organizations that offer therapy, prevention of critical incidents and education, were able to prevent mental health issues. While EAP (Employee Assistance Programs) is reactive in assisting employees struggling with emotional issues, companies' HR departments frequently request them to give talks, presentations and workshops on a range of topics like the resolution of conflicts, resilience training negotiation, leadership, and stress management. All are wellness-focused in terms of education. This kind of awareness-based learning can bring lasting benefits for physical and psychological well-being. The subconscious is much more with the body than any other method of interacting with the body. Hypochondriac is a good example of a mental state that can cause disease when physical causes are not evident. By exercising the mind, beliefs, many diseases are made real, just as an illusion can deceive people into thinking that the patient is receiving medical treatment when they're taking a sugar or salt pill and improving. Another instance could be pain caused by stress that leads to stiff joints, neck, or shoulder issues that require chiropractic manipulation to treat the issue, that began as a mental issue. Massage spas are extremely popular that they're now thriving businesses that earn a significant amount of revenue due to muscle tension due to stress in the workplace.

The awareness training can improve both physical and psychological health over the long-term. To create an active wellness program to provide counsel, EAP organizations need to enhance their current offerings in order to be able of convincing executives and HR managers that there's an economic benefit from an emotionally well-balanced, and content-based employee. Naturally, the idea of reducing leavers and absences from work has been promoted by EAP and, in actuality, employees are emotionally supported. This means it is much easier to refer to the employee promptly when a mental disorder is present and keep their jobs longer and longer. However, a wellness component of EAP can decrease the necessity for therapy if employees are taught the mental health knowledge and skills in advance of an incident or have an accident that requires medical attention.

As with physical incentive programs by way of an EAP client program Therapy is more affordable to the average employee. Although it's cheaper than physical wellness to see a private psychologist, many individuals have done. The first thing to remember is that there are three motives to see a psychologist: you're facing an emergency and require assistance, and lastly, you're feeling lost and have no direction and would like to consider the possibilities that are available for your life and your choices for the future. This third factor can be thought of as a holistic approach to psychology. Additionally, they could go one step further by providing individuals with awareness-based coaching and education to be proactive and will help prevent the development of mental health issues in the future by providing people with the tools needed now to be more adaptable and ready to deal with life's emotional fluctuations and ups and downs. Many employees who have undergone the leadership and awareness training or endurance training could be better able to identify the signs of mental health issues prior to they develop into medical issues which require treatment.

Psychological wellbeing and its application What is the best way to make psychological well-being function? From the first moment there is a tiny issue. Just similar to a physical wellness check-up. In the event that you do, you'll always have something wrong which requires attention prior to registering for the wellness program in any way. It is extremely unlikely that any person who chooses to go through a psycho-wellness package will experience no difficulties in the least. A series of counselling sessions will, therefore, need been scheduled to address present emotional issues that may have been dealt with in the past. Another possibility is that, once an assessment of psychological health is conducted it could reveal problems that have been lingering for a long period of time, and are now being brought to the mind's eye. You should be completely free of any emotional troubles, be it in the previous (depression) or the current (work and at home) or even the near future (cognition-provoking anxiousness). Psychological wellness and wellness could be a good starting point for mentally bringing anyone to an equilibrium before any wellness program is a viable option.

It is crucial to consider the counseling and health programs in the context of the key to achieving for good mental health. Health in the physical sense is costly as well as inclusive in the sense that only the wealthy with high net worth can have the luxury of the benefits of a wellness plan for the duration of their lives. However, in terms of psychological health it is a different story. EAP and the coaching and training and insight counseling could be a positive influence on the future health of your mind with a low cost. In addition, helping to improve psychological health as a method of ensuring good management for reducing absences and leavers can be very cost-effective for businesses. The expense of replacing employees is significantly higher than the worth that comes from an EAP contract that is of high quality. To those who are not, speaking to a psychiatrist or a performance counsellor, psychotherapist even if you're not suffering from an issue with your mental health at the moment, if your current state is more resilient in the present and you're able to pay back dividends in the future for issues that could be prevented. An understanding of your style, personality and characteristics will help you make sense of your life. Well-being and psychological preparation for a best future be a perfect match.

In self-interest that is rational, certain economic decisions are made. However, they don't start to encompass the entire amount of the economic decisions made by people.

None of these is the most convincing argument in support of the idea that every economic decision is driven by rational self-interest. It's the fact that the majority of products that are bought are not because of their value, but due to the effectiveness of advertising. The best product could be purchased by a buyer motivated by rational self-interest but over and over again with Beta and VS, with the mom and pop shops. Fast food chains-we can see the market gaining with an inferior product. The reason fast food chains dominate the market is because their suppliers are more adept in marketing. However, marketing-based decisions aren't decisions based on reason. We are making decisions based on emotion.

What is the reason these decisions are cognitively on? Since that's what the majority of advertising campaigns are trying to achieve. There are very few ads that demonstrate the advantages of the product clearly and in a rational manner. They make use of all kinds of psychological methods to convince people to buy the product. Marketing rarely focuses on reason only; it is a game that plays on the people's emotions often, making this feeling the basis that is manipulated by the marketing professional.

Does this make all the choices made by people in their economic decisions incorrect? But what it does show is that a lot of these decisions aren't founded on what is believed as the basis of economic theory from the past. Does that mean capitalism is dead? the indefinability on one of the fundamental principles. There are certainly economical choices based on self-interest that are rational However, there are a lot of economic choices that are not or logical, and it is essential to think about these matters whether you're an individual consumer, producer or a decision-maker.

In his own way the customer must be aware of psychology in order that advertisers aren't so susceptible to manipulation by psychological means. The policymaker would like to know the areas where people make money and what they should to do to prevent criminal practices. Honest producers such as Borland and other mom-and-pop stores need to be aware of the ways in which their competitors use deceitful techniques for advertising and then react by themselves with a successful and intelligent marketing. I'm not a fan of communism. I advocate capitalism that is moral. That means, most of all, recognizing the ways in which people are being deceived and ending the corrupt practices in economics which make them look foolish.

Of course, a lot of the blame is on the customer themselves, who usually do not think or are dumb. Some of these issues are solved through broad-based education that helps people develop more rational thinking habits to make it so easy to make use of these in the same way as exercising more freedom and be accountable in their choices regarding their finances. The more decisions are based on rational interests and the more the economy is functioning as it should; however, the more manipulative psychology that they focus on as the economy becomes a reckless and corrupt system that treats people like fools and laughs at the bank.

At a minimum the clarification of this issue is vital. A flawed theory is one that fails to recognize an extensive portion of the factors that influence the purchasing choices of individuals. It is important to examine and recognize the importance of psychology in the consumer's decision-making for the majority of decisions made by consumers that it is responsible for. On this basis it's then possible to establish whether economic practices contribute to the good of the population and which methods of economics aren't. It is at a minimum that this information is crucial. A flawed theory is one that fails to recognize many of the motives behind the purchase decisions of individuals. It is important to examine and recognize the role played by psychology in the making of decisions by consumers for the majority of the consumer's decisions that it is accountable for. Based on this it's then possible to establish whether economic practices contribute to the good of the population and which ones aren't.

The second chapter is about myths concerning

body language

A reputable veterinarian can confirm, when you're checking pets and discussing with their owner, making the right diagnosis is the most important thing. With your team in charge, leading complicated procedures is not a problem. While you might be on the job in hand or the conversation going on you are also taking note of the non-verbal communications of the people who are around you. Be it consciously or unconsciously the ability to read body language clearly is a requirement for an effective professional, particularly in the field of veterinary medicine.

You can determine something about how people behave. The tense hands of a new vet technician or the bulging eyes of a patient will tell you much about the situation, without communication. While some non-verbal signals are simple to discern however, you may be unintentionally misjudging an event or even a person by the way they look based on myths about body language you believe to be accurate.

You might need to reconsider your thinking. Here are some of the most common body language signals which you might be interpreting wrong.

Myth #1: Liars don't make eye contact.
The Truth: It's likely to be more prevalent for children of a young age not to make eye contact while they are lying but it is a habit that many people either get rid of or control later in life, especially in the event that they become adept at lying. In reality, people might not be inclined to eye contact because they're anxious or have a limited attention span, or simply because it's culturally acceptable to avoid eye contact.

Myth 2: Arms crossed indicate anger or resistance.
The truth: A person who has their arms crossed may be communicating a range of things. Can resistance to the situation be one of the signs? Yes, absolutely. However, crossed arms can be a sign of anxiety or nervousness. Many people turn towards crossed arms, or an "self-hug" to relieve stress. for stress reduction. People also cross their arms in difficult situations to protect them from whatever they are feeling anxious about. It's not unusual to see people mirror their actions to others during conversations. Have you crossed

your arms? This could be a quick indication that the person you're chatting has arm crossed, too.

Myth 3 that hands moving while talking can be a sign of unease.
The Truth: Although excessive fidgeting is the way that some people react when they feel uncomfortable, hand gestures are often necessary to convey the message. This is particularly relevant when the client is explaining the symptoms his pet's behavior is showing and may require gestures at specific body parts. Then, the client might take a look at your hand gestures in order to follow and understand the condition you're describing.

Chapter 3: Cues That Say It All Context Overrides Words

In all cultures there are facial expressions that break down any cultural barriers. Researchers find that all around the world emotions like sadness, happiness shock, fear, anger, and disgust are expressed in the same way. The act of gesturing, which can also be described as touching can send out certain signals that aid in expressing emotions.

Nonverbal communication, however, essentially is taking a look at the text and finding truth in the language. A person could be saying something however their tone could mean different things to someone else. Researchers have put non-verbal communication into five types. Let's look at them all.

1. Repetition

If you are in a conversation It is beneficial to repeat what another person said to increase memory. If someone repeats verbally the words you spoke to them, they're showing that your words are important. They should be prepared to be able to access the information in the future.

Also, this could be taken as a sign that they're noting the words you're using. Be careful, however because a lot of repetition could cause aggravation for certain. They'll interpret your cues since this is what mothers often give their children when they begin to speak.

2. Contradiction

Contradiction is among the most obvious signals that indicate rejection. In many cases such subtle contradictions could be used to denigrate the other or signal the power of one. One of the first instances of this occurs in the workplace. A controlling manager listens to her employee's conversation to a customer. The customer is asking for a few questions regarding a specific procedures. The employee is trying to give a more elegant explanation to meet her objective. When she hears this the manager's response, he immediately intervenes, telling the employee that her approach is not correct and proceeds to guide the customer. Imagine how the employee felt. She was not only embarrassment in front of a client however, her professionalism was challenged. The customer was prompted to view the employee as someone who's not well-educated. The supervisor could have handled the situation in more elegant fashion but, it's certain that it was done in the desire to demonstrate the superiority of his position.

3. Substitutions

Do you remember the look that your mother gave you when she said she believed the words she spoke of? Most likely, you'll remember those sharp eyes, a unruly mouth, and the exaggerated manner of speaking. Your mom didn't have to speak a word for you to realize that your behavior was unacceptable. We use daily substitutes to express our feelings. The intense glares or the slight glances can be a powerful signal to those who are familiar with one another. They also signify the emphasis of the particular request. Dogs are primarily able to communicate via vocalisations. If you stare at the dog and say "Back," they know the area is not accessible to them. The specific word is substituted for a specific move.

4. Complensating

If a kid does admirably in his sports and is noticed by the crowd, they can spot the coach rubbing his back or giving him a high-five. These gestures of appreciation outwardly are well-known signals that indicate the accomplishment of a job well done. It could be a smile or hand gesture or perhaps an embrace to convey our pride sentiments towards others. This gentle sign of approval can be seen in both gender roles too. Footballers are frequently noticed rubbing their butts on their fellow players to indicate a job good job. If they are in a relationship, it could be an invitation to sexual intimacy.

5. Accenting

It happens when people want to be heard. They'll bang their doors when they shout a comment or shake their hands in a stoic manner. It's like accentuating a particular word. This tiny dash will bring accent to one or more of the mentioned letters. It also warns the reader of a change in their pronunciation. In the same way, accenting nonverbal signals could indicate an adjustment in behaviour. When looking at people who have deep-seated fears, they'll rely in large part on the accent of their speech in order to appear dominant. They're trying to create anxiety in their subject as a method to gain control.

Gestures can help to enhance conversations and create the conversation more exciting. People who make use of gestural gestures can be described as "people who speak with hand gestures." The gestures can enhance the storyline of a tale or help to lighten a discussion. They're descriptive and they are prone to catching the attention of the audience or even a private. Speechmaking classes put a great amount of emphasis on the necessity of using gestures during their delivery. They add emotion to the words being said, and add a sense of urgency. One of the most effective ways to build a sense of connection is to touching. The warm embrace of an acquaintance or a loved one can ease stress and create an atmosphere of belonging. When you're grieving, sometimes the words of well-meaning people do not suffice. A slur of a hand says, "I am here for you," during a way which words cannot ever express. The reasoning behind this is that touching is an act. It is a way of showing your enthusiasm for them. Furthermore, touching hands could be a sign of a person's character. Certain managers evaluate candidates based on the way they shake hands. If they are greeted with an unsteady handshake and the boss is able to feast on their shy nature. They'll be reluctant to hire their employees in a frantic environment. In contrast the firm shake oozes confidence. The hiring manager could be drawn to the candidate since they didn't show any anxiety.

In different cultures, the amount of privacy differs across different cultures. East Asian cultures typically stand approximately one to two inches away of the individual they are interacting with. This is a sign of respect and curiosity. In the United States, however it is possible to view proximity to space as intrusive. It is possible that we are uneasy about what the individual's intentions are. But, creating an over quantity of space could lead your spouse to believe that you shouldn't be with them. A well-balanced view of space is essential to effectively communicate. Look at what space is between point of your pointer finger and the inner elbow. This is typically the best amount of space that will allow you to speak easily with your partner.

The way the person speaks can also indicate the character traits of a person. Teachers in grammar schools typically are known to speak to their students with high-pitched sounds, since it creates excitement and is appealing. But, that kind of excitement may not be appropriate at an all-adult event. If someone attempted to speak to another adult in this manner the adult who was receiving it could think that the person is was being rude. It's important to think about the tone in which you're talking so that you do not appear unprofessional, rude or even flirty. A balanced approach to talking while incorporating inflections as required will allow you to effectively communicate without causing offense. Communication that is nonverbal can be learned by studying simple signals that are present in every day. You'll think, "When someone speaks to me this way How does it feel?" Or, "Am I comfortable with the fact that someone is in front of myself?" By asking yourself these questions, you'll be able to communicate effectively with other people and learn from their signals.

How can you evaluate the behavior of people? Ability to understand people can greatly influence how you handle them. If you know the way someone feels, you can alter your message and communication method to ensure you are receiving it in the most effective way. What are you paying attention to? What other clues might hint at what they are thinking or experiencing? If you're reading your boss, colleague or your partner, to comprehend the people you meet, you have to let go of the biases of your mind, and some walls have to be thrown down. While the brain is as brilliant as it is, you must be willing to give up outdated, restrictive ideas. People who can read other people well have been trained to discern the unnoticed. They've learned to use abilities to go beyond where you normally focus your focus to gain life-changing intuition knowledge. Studies have shown that language is 7 percent of the way we communicate, while our body language, 55 percent and voice tone percent represent the remaining. In this case, the thing to consider is letting off the pressure to discern body language. Avoid becoming overly focused or analytic. Keep your mind relaxed and relaxed. Sit back, relax and be aware.

1. Pay attention to appearance

While reading other people's posts, take note of whether they are wearing an outfit with a high-end suit and polished shoes, dressed to succeed with a sense of determination? Jeans and a t-shirt that show the ease of being casual? A tight, cleavage-lined top is a beautiful option?

2. Notice Posture

If you are observing someone's posture, consider whether they are holding their heads high and confident? Do they walk with a sluggishness or squirm, which is a sign of self-doubt? Do they flaunt an over-inflated chest, which is a sign of an ego-driven person?

3. Be aware of physical movements
Distance and leaning. Be aware of the places where people lean. We tend to lean towards those we enjoy but away from the ones that we do not. Legs and arms crossed is an expression of defense, anger or self-defense. When people cross their legs, they are likely to turn the toes of their upper leg toward the person they feel most comfortable with.

* Keeping one hand - If people put their hands on pockets, laps, or even behind their backs, it implies that they're concealing something.

* Cuticle biting or lip biting When people bit or lick their lips or pick at their cuticles,, they attempt to relax their stress or to ease an uncomfortable situation.

4. Interpret Facial Expression
The emotions we feel can be etched onto our faces. Deep frown lines can indicate anxiety or overthinking. The crow's feet are lines of happiness. Lips that have been puffed up signal displeasure, anger, or bitterness. Teeth that are clenched and jaws grinding can be a sign of tension.

Expressions of emotions are stunning. They are the manifestation of our energy, the "vibe" we emit. They are interpreted by our the senses. Certain people are comfortable to be around. They increase your energy and mood. Others can be draining and you want to run away. The "subtle energy" is felt by inches or feet away from your body, even though it's invisibly. In Chinese medicine, it's known as Chi, which is a vitality crucial for health.

1. Feel People's Presence

This is the general energy we release that is not always in line with the words we use or our actions. It's the emotional environment that surrounds us, like a cloud of rain or sun. When you read, people will notice whether they are an attractive, friendly appearance that draws you? Are you feeling the willies that make you turn away?

2. Watch People's Eyes

The eyes are a powerful source of energy. Similar to the brain having an electromagnetic signal that extends out over the entire body research suggest that the eyes emit the same signals. Pay attention to eye movements of people. Are they looking at you with concern? Are they sexually attractive? Are they cruel? Do they seem angry?

Find out if there is an individual at home in their eyes, which suggests the possibility of intimacy? Do they appear to be a bit secluded or evading?

3. Be aware of the feeling of an Handshake, Hug and even touching

We exchange emotional energy through physical contact, much like the electrical energy. Consider, does the touch of a hug or handshake feel warm, relaxed or secure? Are they off-putting enough that you're ready to leave? Do you notice that people's hands are clammy signifying an anxiety? Are they limp, suggesting that they are uncommittal and hesitant?

4. Watch for Tone of voice and laugh

The volume and tone of our voice tell many things about our moods. Sound waves create vibrations. When you read someone, pay attention to how their voice affects your. Do you think the tone seem soothing? Is it harsh or snippy?

The mouth is a language that needs to be decoded

If someone is smiling, it's an excellent sign, isn't it? Not necessarily. Different smiles can mean different things. Same goes regarding the angle of someone's lips.

1. Smiles

* When you smile with a authentic smile the

corners of your mouth open upwards and the eyes are widened and become wrinkled around the corners.

Smiles that are genuine generally do not have to do with the eyes. They may happen due to discomfort.

A smirk, or even a partial smile following an expression of displeasure or displeasure can signal the presence of doubt, disdain or displeasure.

A smile that is accompanied by constant gaze, prolonged look, or even a head tilt may indicate the attraction.

2. Lips

A narrowed or compressed lips could indicate unease.

Lips that are twitchy can indicate sadness or anxiety.

* Lips with a purported grin can signal displeasure or anger.

* Partly open, but slightly open lips usually indicate that people feel relaxed or at relaxed.

The eyes are the code for decoding

Eyes convey many details about a person's attitude and level of curiosity.

1. Blinking

People often blink fast during times of tension. It

is possible that blinking fast can indicate deceit, but that's not always the case.

The blinking of a person could speed up while they're:

* tackling a challenging issue
* Feeling uneasy
* concerned or scared of something

2. Pupil dilation

Your pupils tend to expand when you are feeling positive toward someone or something. The feelings could be romance, but it's not always the situation. The dilation is triggered by the stimulation of the nervous system. Therefore, it's possible to notice dilation in pupils when you're scared or angry. If you aren't happy with certain things, the pupils typically shrink, or become smaller.

3. Gaze direction

Eyes tend to focus on the things you're interested in So observing the movements of someone's eyes can provide you with insight into their mood.

If you're speaking to someone who's eyes are constantly wandering towards the buffet table it is possible that they have an interest more in food rather than conversing at present. People who are looking to the exit might want to go out.

People are also prone to shift their eyes to the side when they:
* tackling the issue
* Recalling information or memories
* thinking about something that is difficult

4. Eye blockage
* Blocking is a term used to describe things like:
* cover your eyes with a glove
* close your eyes for a few seconds for example, in an extended blink
* rubbing your eyes
* blinking

Blocking is usually inconspicuous, but it does tend to indicate how you feel. People tend to put their eyes in a corner when they're angry or upset, or confronted by something they don't like doing. It could also indicate discord or resistance. It is obvious that the house requires an overhaul however, if your spouse proposes a day off for chores, you could appear to be a bit tense before you realize.

5. Pay attention to the legs and arms
While people typically utilize their legs and arms to perform a specific gesture actions that occur more naturally can be a good indicator of emotions.

1. Arms

Many people do this when they are feeling:
* vulnerable
* nervous
* not interested in considering a different viewpoint

It is interesting to note that crossed arms also indicate confidence. If one crosses their arms smile, leaning back or other indications of calm and relaxed, they are likely to feel at ease with the situation rather than being vulnerable. Arms may also give people a sense of security. Be on the lookout for any of the following behaviors:
* placing something in the chest
* placing an arm on a table or chair
* stretching an arm to create distance
* with one arm used to support the other in the back

These movements subconsciously signal that the person isn't fully at ease with the situation and requires stability or secure themselves in some manner.

2. The feet and legs

The legs and feet can be a source of anxiety and restlessness:
* tapping feet
* leg jiggling

The foot is moved from side to side

A crossed leg can also signal that you are not interested in what someone is saying particularly when arms are crossed. The feet can also provide details. Take note of the direction that someone's feet are facing in a conversation. If their feet are pointed away, they might think that they are leaving the conversation rather than continuing. If their feet are pointed towards you, they are likely to be enjoying the conversation and hopes to keep it going.

3. Hands

A lot of people make gestures to emphasis when they speak. This has advantages directly, and research by researchTrusted Source suggests that people tend to respond to someone's question more quickly if we perform gestures when they ask questions. The more enthusiastic the gestureis, the greater excitement someone is likely to be experiencing. It's also quite common for people to make gestures towards those they feel close to, sometimes without even realizing it.

Here are some additional items to look out for:
* Hands outstretched with palms facing upwards could be a subconscious reflection of an openness.
The clenched fists of a fist can indicate an anger

or frustration particularly for those who are trying to control these feelings. You may notice that the expression of their face remains unconstrained, perhaps even relaxed.

The instinctive touch on the cheek could indicate that someone is examining something with care or has lots of curiosity about the topic you're discussing.

Breathing signals

The frequency of your breathing can pick up when you're feeling stressed. The stress could be positive or negative therefore a person who breathes fast could be:

* Excited
* worried
* anxious or nervous

A deep, long breath could suggest:

* Relief
* anger
* fatigue

The slower breathing patterns typically indicate the state of mind or contemplation. Normal breathing patterns might not be noticed as much but a person's breathing may appear extremely precise or controlled. This kind of intentional control usually occurs in the course of trying to control the intensity of a feeling for example, anger.

When assessing body positions
The way someone sits or stands and how they position themselves will give you clues to how they're feeling.

1. Posture
The way you stand, and how you stand isn't always easy for you to control, and could make it difficult to comprehend. But it could provide insights, particularly if it is different from how people generally behave. There are some signs to be looking for:
Leaning against the wall or any other support could suggest disinterest or boredom.
* Leaning into conversations or in a direction towards someone generally indicates an interest or enthusiasm.
Standing straight, often holding hands to hips could suggest excitement, enthusiasm and confidence.
Standing straight with hands on both sides, is a popular posture that indicates the willingness to engage and listen.
* Resting the head with one hand may show an interest. If both hands are supporting your head

in any way, this could indicate fatigue or boredom.

The tilting of the body or head to one side indicates the presence of attention and focus. It may also signal attraction, based on the other body language signals.

2. Distance

The amount of physical distance that a person keeps when they talk to you may reveal their mood or their feelings towards you. Be aware that a lot of people prefer to maintain their distance from other people, especially those whom they do not know. However certain people might be at ease with less privacy. They might stand or even sit close, as this is how they are used to interacting.

However, certain specific actions can indicate:

* Anyone who is regularly standing or is very near to you is likely to enjoy your company.

Someone who is distinct and steps back when you move forward is likely to wish to keep the separation (physical or emotionally) away from.

* Being close enough to touch or engaging in a conversation especially with a smile or even a small touch usually implies physical attraction.

* Holding up an arm or hand when taking a step back frequently indicates a desire to create an

physical barrier or distance.

Summary

Language can be complicated and difficult to comprehend. In actual fact there's a whole area of study, referred to as Kinesics, that focuses on understanding the non-verbal language. A slight shift in posture or shifts in facial expressions are commonplace over the course of conversation or social exchange. However, someone who has an unabated posture or static expression could be making a great deal of effort in order to block their true feelings from revealing. If you're having a difficult to understand the body language of a person, consider these guidelines in your mind:

• Speak to them. It's never a bad idea to inquire about how someone else feel. If you see a restless foot or fists that are clenched Try removing them and asking if all is right.

Take note of their previous body language. The way that people communicate can differ from one person to another. If a person's body language suddenly appears different, it's an indication that something is happening beneath the surface.

* Try to achieve a certain level in eye contact. It's not necessary to stare or keep eyes, however it will assist to look at someone's eyes and keep it

for the duration of a conversation. Additionally, it's easier to recognize the body language of someone when you're paying attention to the person.

Be sure to pay attention. Good communication always involves listening. Don't get involved in trying to figure out the movements or gestures of someone that you don't pay attention to their words.

In general, you cannot discern the way people feel and think through their body language on its own. If you consider your body language in its context with their language, you can receive more information than you do when you consider each type of communication on its own.

Here are 8 additional tips on for reading other people:

1. Establish an initial baseline

People are different in their quirks and behaviors. For instance, they may clean their throats, gaze at the floor when they talk or cross their arms. They may also scratch their heads, rub their necks, squint, and jiggle their feet often. At first, we might not even be aware that others are doing these behaviors. In the event that we are aware, won't pay attention to it. People exhibit these behaviors for a variety of motives. It could be a matter of manners. Sometimes, though they can be a sign of deceit or even anger or nervousness. Establishing a mental picture of the normal behavior of others can help you greatly.

2. Look for deviations

Take note of the inconsistencies that exist between the foundation you've set and the individual's words and gestures. As an example, you've observed that a major supplier is known to clear his throat frequently when he's stressed. After introducing some minor changes to your business arrangement, he will begin to perform this. Are there more to this than what you initially think? You may decide to investigate further, asking extra questions you usually.

3. Watch for the clusters of gestures

A single gesture or word can be a sign of any thing, but when a variety of behavior blunders are joined be aware. For instance, not only is your provider constantly clear of his throat however, he is also doing the head scratching thing. And he continues to shuffle his feet. Be careful.

4. Compare and contrast

Okay, you've noticed that someone's behavior seems differently than usual. Increase your focus an notch to check what happens if the individual does the same thing with the other members of your group. Be sure to watch the person as they interact with the other members of the group. Do you notice a change in the expression of the person? What is the impact on his or her body language and posture?

5. Take a look at the mirror.

Mirror neurons are the built-in monitors inside our brains, which mirror the state of other people's mind. We are wired to recognize the body language of others. Smiles activate the muscles that smile on our own faces, whereas an expression of frown stimulates our muscles of frown. When we meet someone we like, our eyebrows sway and the facial muscles relax. the head tilts and blood flow into our lips and fills them. If your partner isn't receptive to the same behavior, they might be conveying a message clearly that they don't like you , or isn't satisfied with what you've done.

6. Find the voice that is strong

Most powerful people isn't always the person at the top on the other side of the table. People who are confident have powerful voices. When seated at a table for a conference the most confident person is likely to be the strongest one with a wide posture, a powerful voice, and large smile. If you're pitching your idea to an audience, it's simple to focus on the person who is the leader of the group. However, the leader might have a negative personality. In the real world, he relies heavily on others to make the decisions as well as being easily affected their decisions. Recognize the powerful voice and your odds of success will increase significantly.

7. Watch how they walk.

It is common for people to shuffle through life, have no flow of movement in their actions, or do not keep their heads down are not confident in themselves. If you observe these characteristics on someone on your team, you may try to give them a kudos in order to boost confidence in the person. It is also possible to ask them more specific questions in the course of a meeting, to help to bring those brilliant ideas to the forefront.

8. Find clues to your personality

Everyone has a distinct personality There are some basic information that will allow you to understand someone else, so that you can understand the person's personality accurately.

* Does anyone exhibit more of an introverted or more extroverted personality?

* Does he/she appear to be motivated by

significance or relationships?
* How do they manage the uncertainty and risk?
* What feeds his the self-esteem?
What are the person's behaviours when stressed?
What are the person's behavior when they are at ease?
She acknowledges that it takes time to understand how to read people clearly. Naturally you will find exceptions to each rule. However, keeping these rules in mind while you develop your ability to observe will significantly improve the ability of you to comprehend people as well as understand their thought processes and be able to communicate effectively.

Chapter 4: Various Methods Of Connecting

There are many ways and methods when communicating with each other. It is no doubt that speaking in words is probably the most well-known of all. Sometimes, the words are not only sufficient or vital in conveying thoughts. In such situations the body language is a factor. Often, people express their most intimate feelings through their body language, this is why it must be dealt with.

It is evident that many people attempt in improving the way they speak but without being aware of what exactly it is about. If you are looking to try to improve the part of your personality that you are displaying and improve your communication skills, you must be aware of the same. You can find out more about this specific non-verbal skill by studying and comprehending it. It is generally believed that it's a part of the just the body's movements but it's not true. It's much more, and encompasses a range of elements like the formation of eyes, external appearances signals, and some other things.

At this point, you are aware that body language is in daily life all the time. This means that you can be aware that body language is crucial in the world of social interaction and you must understand its significance. Different experts pondered the significance of this form of non-verbal communication, and came up with different conclusions and interpretations. For instance, one analyst named John Borg said that personal communication is made up of 93% non-verbal signals, such as movements, appearances and body postures. The remainder of the 7% communicated via the use of words or verbal communications.

If you've gotten the importance of non-verbal communication within the public it is time to get serious about it. In addition to increasing your skills in this area, you must be able to read how body language is used by others also. This is extremely helpful in understanding what the other person is trying to communicate. Additionally, it aids in determining how someone responds to your conversation.

There are many who like to look at the appearances of other people and try to learn their culture. It is your duty to follow suit and be grateful for it.

The way you speak to others is an important aspect of communicating your advantages or receptivity. Also, the eye-to-eye contact and a smile is a significant. In any event, what are the various types of messages you can convey to let someone on the opposite gender know that they are attractive to you? Your posture, the way you place your body with respect to them, how you interact with them, and even your outward appearance are ways to convey your receptivity or absence of engagement.

For you to think of how these variables work to form an either-or I'll give you an example.

Imagine that someone is trying to grab your attention and you discover that the person is completely incongruous. You are not enthused by the person in any way however, in reality you want the person to not bother you. What can you do to spread the message without encouraging the person to go off on their own?

It is recommended to stay off eye-to-eye contact. You might look at the individual's shoulder in a specific spot above the area, or even turn your head away. You could possibly lower your body slightly and fold your arms around your chest. You should avoid conversation by reacting only when it is necessary or necessary, then following up simply saying either or.

Even the most dense person would ignore the message. Your body language says everything, and without a word being spoken.

Your body language could convey positive energy and a feeling of openness, or signal to people to stay away. Arms crossed can mean "I'm struggling and I need to be secure," or, "I'm not open to you. Please stay far from my side."

If you want to appear friendly and friendly, don't put your arms down. Move your jaw slightly to appear more relaxed and straighten your shoulders to show people that you're cautious and ready to get to know them.

If someone is bending their legs or arms when

you walk by or if someone is sitting down with their shoulders down and their head slumped, that could indicate that the person is not friendly.

One woman was at an annual Christmas party hoping to meet new people and was unable to understand why no one spoke to her. One month later, after her friend displayed photos of the event, she realized why no one had moved towards her. The photos showed her slumped in the back of the chair, with her arms folded and jaw closed. The woman was shocked to see the negative impression her posture had created.

From that point she made it a point not to lift her head closed while keeping her arms in an open position, and she smiled and looked around at any it was that she could see someone she wanted to meet.

Body Language Training

In all cases, is it better to understand and use the ability? What is the best method to master non-verbal communication? Check out these motivating signals...

The current excitement for body language training is a fantastic beginning!
A quick search of Google or YouTube concerning the subject of body language will reveal a wealth of important information that will allow you to gain knowledge on this fascinating topic. A large number of people are demonstrating how to observe the effects of certain movements. Many are beginning to realize how to control their posture and arms to create more impact. Learning the fundamentals in body language are starting to form the basis of the new age of communication, in which everything happens very quickly. But, we may be able to show the things that are missing.

The body Language Expert

If you take classes for long enough, you could obtain a doctorate degree in the field you are interested in and, in the long run, it will qualify you as an expert. However:

How much expertise do you currently possess with its application?

What type of impression do you get from the

effect your subject's influence has on others?

How often do you implement the information you have about yourself and the way you conduct yourself?

The same way that the possession of a driver's license will not mean you are a professional when you're driving or knowing how to put your hands up makes you an expert in non-verbal communication. It could be misinterpreted. But, it's implied as an attempt to get past the process of learning and truly get to know what's going on.

Understanding the body's language

Today being a professional implies that you know your subject in order to gain any discussion. But, imagine a situation that completing a task without fail requires an entirely new approach to understand your subject in all its aspects, is a good idea to use the concept. Think about your possibilities that this nil distinction here is in connection with your enthusiasm. Imagine a scenario in which you combine your knowledge and what you believe is the most important thing. This is where you'll be in a state of uncertainty. It could also be the time to begin your first steps into the realm of authority through body language. Be cautious, but this method is likely to require you to research further.

"Know Youself and Understand The Universe"

Moving beyond the realm of skills to the realm of authority, you must be willing to discover the inner you. It is a matter of practicing to acquire knowledge into the connection you have with your body language and emotions associated with every posture or movement. In a way, we individuals are alike. Similar to how PC programming is performed by "stacks," beginning with the machine code level, which is comprised of ones or zeros. So too are we. For us, those numbers and zeros that are symbolic can refer to happiness/torment, joy/happiness or even dis-ease for a few examples. It is important to find out what is fulfilling the need to feel more relaxed and comfortable than ever before, and you can determine what isn't. Then you need to connect your feelings with the body language. Then, you must focus on connecting your experiences and emotions in order to recognize any connection with similar body language patterns seen in others. This requires you to master difficult skills.

Does it be a problem?
Similar to the process of scavenging through an unclean and dusty storage area looking into how you look and the emotions associated with it may appear to be difficult, and even dangerous. The main reason that the majority of us are hesitant from engaging in this process is because it's not uncommon to uncover recollections and emotions that you have ignored or hid. The process of shedding light on these things can be a challenge and can be a bit painful. However keeping with the process until the end is a great feeling. It requires a lot of energy to cement those old memories created. In a few places they become hardened to the point where muscles can feel similar to ligaments or bone. But for every complicated problem you discover and deal with your problem, the energy that you used to ensure it was solidified is released. You'll be able to apply it much more efficiently. What could you do to do to increase your energy within your own life?

Another aspect that is uplifting about this is that

because we are all made up in a way that is moderately in the future, you'll realize that other people suffer from similar issues in similar regions of their bodies as you do. Imagine a scenario where this is how we get our most profound compassions.

Making connections that last

If you're fortunate enough to have someone who is able to connect with you with compassion, then you will feel how wonderful and liberating it is. It is also evident how happy, light and bubbly your body is in the after you have invested your energy in them. You also realize the attractiveness of them and how eagerly you anticipate returning to them. However, regardless of whether this kind person is not aware of body language communication, see whether you are able to detect their awareness and the intense feeling you get from being around someone. You might be able to use this method to:

Be a leader in a way that you choose and value what follows?

Selling and presenting in a way that enables this

perception?

Serving others with a way that builds trust with clients.

Are you able to create a totally irresistible type of friendship?

Be a better parent or father?

Authority, using the most effective equalization of both information and

Imagine a scenario where one people are able to analyze body language with thrilling and delicate abilities, its effect is the assurance of the subsequent period of body language that is prepared. The act of examining body language is similar to studying a motion control. It's a scientific process which often leads experts to debate with one another about what they are reading. Does it make sense to say that it's not an entirely different experience when you go to the places that you've read about or see all the attractions, smells of the city, the bustle the sensations, the preferences and the feelings it triggers?

Academic ability is exceptional but, deliberately tackling actual situations is much more impressive. Begin with us in this manner where you feel open!
What else are you accomplished with a high level of non-verbal communication?

Have you ever thought about what kind of information is available from your body, how important that it can be, as well as who could access it? Did you know that there is an increasing desire for profiting from the process of figuring out the ways to interpret this unexplored part of our human behaviour? What are the benefits and outcomes of this particular pattern?

The use of body language in the workplace can be a powerful tool to enhance relationships.

One of the major goals that has been a major focus of Information Age has been on improving efficiency and making interactions efficient. Because of the ubiquitous use of technology, practically every business practice hasn't been revamped or redesigned. While, excitement and dismay are not spared by the integration of computers and machines into our lives and even work, this glaring focus on mechanical systems could make us uninformed about the information our bodies synthesize and transmit. The body language we use can sometimes contradict or even degrade the message our well-practiced words convey. But, how aware of it are you? of this in the event of an incident?

The power and the security of gravity

For instance, the typical personal interaction with gravity is extremely effective. We tend to underestimate the power of this concept. In reality, who has the capability to think about gravity when there are bills to be paid and items to sell and people to be met? But, think about how revolutionary gravity's appeal holds our reality in place. It holds our moon high. Then, you are free to explore the awe-inspiring quantity of energy a huge majority of us utilize to fight this inexplicably powerful power. Consider for a moment the difference we'd experience and what energy we'd be able to expend, and how much more effectively communication could be achieved by being aware and being more influenced through the force of Gravity?

We pay nearly nothing at all to think about the effectiveness of how that we can achieve by adjusting our posture to the force of gravity. Because interest is a necessary element of our human nature It shouldn't take long before we come back to reap the benefits of increasing effectiveness of non-verbal communication. Think about the possibility that that time has been outlined in this article.

Perusing Body Language Basics

Walk around in a crowded area and observe other people and how they apply their positions to:

- Stand or walk as you incline forward, in reverse, or to the opposite side, and help to neutralize gravity.

- Lean their heads either in the forward or reverse direction, clearly off from their centre of gravity.

- Move your body between sides as you walk ahead.

They should point their feet to an alternative path to the one they're moving towards.

"Wave their arms around much more than simply to keep their arms equal

Shuffle so often as they walk that their shoes wear unevenly

Each of these developments needs the utmost energy and determination to take away the power gravity forces on them. In addition, you should notice that children make the most of gravity however, as we grow older and grow more sophisticated and more sophisticated, we'll, in general, overlook gravity's influence to a growing degree. Making use of one's energy to combat gravity is a waste of time and a complete waste when we're trying to make the most of our lives. If we're that ignorant of the actions of our bodies and how we are affecting our posture, what kind of impact, conscious or unaware, might this behaviour have on those who we're communicating?

The light is on, and no one's home.

Consider how the most important portion of us are ignorant of the actions of our bodies when we are navigating our daily routine. A large portion of these changes result from us not paying attention to our body language, or being trained by society to not notice it. In spite of the benefits or effects that you have, do something consistently to establish the standard of conduct. If you set an example up, it won't take long for it to become to be an element of your identity. For the most significant portion of us, this particular example is incorporated into the person they believe they are. In fact, even with the injury even if the pain you had to stay away from disappears, the instance and muscle strain is often neglected and stays. Some go on to burn through a lot more energy and time complaining about how tired they are. Do you think this is a smart use of our resources?

The use of body language is often not a good sign of.

You're welcome to try giving advice to someone regarding your opinions. If you choose to complete the test, think what reactions you will receive. Many will happily accept the test, and then revert to accusing the test of being a relic. Some will become annoyed that you bring this issue up because it may be "only the way they are." Consider how many people are genuinely grateful for your suggestion and begin making changes to these harmful elements. If you can control information Do you also see an opportunity to get knack of something that others do not?

Reflection over Consciousness and Efficient Body Language

In addition you're welcome to think about what other people's non-verbal communications, personal conduct standards and their responses to your comments can teach you on the individuals including.

Do these instances cause them to appear very attractive?

Do you think you would be very inclined to recruit them?

Do you find yourself fascinated by their recommendation?

Do their experience and age affect the way they respond to you?

Do you want someone from your household to show these kinds of examples?

If not, why not try to do you want to date someone else who is?

Also think about what your reaction reveal about their capability to be interested in, adaptable and responsive?

Why shouldn't you be able to say something about your own body language?

As of now, we've examined the other people who surround you. This is your chance to sit in front of an mirror. Take an attentive review of each of these questions above and see the way they relate to you and your non-verbal communications. What is your body language say about you? What speed would you tell people you would be able to identify and alter it? It is also possible that people around you might be able to see the way forward?

The Benefit of understanding cognizant body language

There's a gold mine in this area waiting for those who are able to read, feel and understand the body language someone else is showing. There's a substantial stake for people who are aware of the meaning of their own body language is saying. There's a third major risk that is awaiting those who understand that by changing their language they will not only be more comfortable and happy, but they'll appear to be more attractive and strong. Does your body language play some connection to your success?

How long would you be able being a non-educated body language?

"What is communication" will surely have crossed the minds of anyone who manages gatherings of colleagues, individuals subordinates, or even the board. It is defined as sharing or trading thoughts emotions, data, or thoughts by writing, speaking or even messages. The ability to communicate requires that you are comfortable with effective methods to convey and acknowledge messages whether written or verbally or by using different kinds of methods. Consider the amount of disagreement that could be kept at in a manner that is strategic to the time saved by not reviewing things again in the event that more focus was put on effectively communicating within the workplace.

Chapter 5: How To Read And Recognize Emotions

Human emotions are the primary main driver behind most of what we think, say and even do. They can be a strong, volatile force inside us, which we often struggle to manage. When someone has learned how to manage not just their own emotions, but also the ability to influence mood of those around them is a sign that they have an extremely superior degree of intelligence.

The most accurate indication of an individual's mood is the facial expressions. Sometimes, these emotions are transferred onto other areas of the body, however facial expressions are the main indication.

In order to be able to discern an individual's mood, consider the expressions on their faces as your initial point of reference. As adults, we tend to attempt to hide our emotions as best we can, especially in the workplace. This is the reason it is so important to observe a person's body language to determine the source of the emotions the individual is feeling.

Humans experience a wide range of emotions, ranging from anger, stress, joy, happiness excitement, exhilaration and many more. They often an accompanying set of signals that are emanating from our bodies. If you are aware of what signs to observe, you'll can identify the emotions of a person.

In order to determine the emotions of a person There are several key indicators to be looking for other than the expression on their face:

* Their voice tone
* Mannerisms
* Deed
* General behavior

Monitoring a person's overall physical health (emotions that are experienced in an extreme way may affect our physical health)

Strategy #17 Strategies #17: Signals of Anger

Perhaps the most straightforward emotion to recognize it is anger. It can be seen in a very clear body language. An expression of deep sigh, eyebrows tightened lips that are tight and thin, fingers pressed together, shoulders tense nostrils swollen as well as a tight jaw and muscles are all indicators of anger in the context of the current emotion that a person is experiencing.

Strategies 18: Signs of Fear

Fear is one of the most basic emotions that trigger the "fight or flight" reaction. It is also easy to detect because a individual's body language can be a dead sign.

If someone is in a state of fear the facial expressions reflect the emotion. The eyes of the person become wide as the fear is clearly evident on the face of the person The mouth is most likely to be opened in out of shock or fear or shock. The lips might tremble nostrils could flare and in certain instances be shivering in sweaty, cold sweats (these sweaty beads usually start appearing at the top of the head).

Strategy #19 The Signs of Deception

Humans can be skilled in deceiving by their words, however the human body is an extremely convincing lie-teller. There are many lies that have the intention of misleading you. If, for instance, someone claims, "Yeah, I'm fine Don't be concerned about it', and they aren't well that may be a attempt to stop you from asking further questions since the person isn't sure about talking about it right now. If someone is lying You must look into the person's behavior and actions after having asked them a question.

If someone is lying the person usually Ignores a question with lengthy explanations or responses without actually discussing the question. If you suspect that someone is not entirely truthful with you, look at the manner of speaking they use to detect the signs of deceit.

Someone who is deceived will rub their nose or face or hide their facial or mouth because it is a method to conceal the truth. The pressure of deceit can cause the skin to become cold and begin itching or even flushing. Be aware when you see someone abruptly scratches their nose or ears. Excessive sweating and avoidance of eye contact are other indications of dishonesty despite the fact that they are speaking exactly what you should listen to.

Strategies #20: Signals that Show Enthusiasm and Joy

If someone is showing expressions of enthusiasm when they are enthusiastic, they tend to smile and move their arms frequently. If you observe people who are extremely passionate about the subjects they're discussing You will see that they are likely to move frequently using their arms. They talk with enthusiasm and move with their arms in order to highlight the points they're making. If someone is excited and content about something, you'll see a lot of smiles when the person is expressing his or her opinion.

Strategy #21 21: Beware of Signs of Unhappiness

The feeling of being unhappy can be strong emotional emotion that is difficult to conceal. If someone is unhappy having a dialogue with you you'll observe that the person's feet and upper body look in a different direction from the conversation, signalling the person's internal desire to stop the conversation as their thoughts are focused focussed on something else. They may also exhibit an uninvolved body and arms crossed across their chests, shoulders slumped and a downward gaze to indicate their feelings of sadness.

Let's talk about emotional intelligence since it's an essential component of understanding people's feelings.

Improving Your Emotional Intelligence

In addition to utilising the body language indicators mentioned above to identify the fundamental emotions we experience Another thing you can try is to develop the ability to recognize emotions. If you can learn to spot and understand emotions (not only in people around you but also within yourself) You will be able engage with someone emotionally at a deeper personal level.

Since you are able to be able to empathize with

and understand the motivations of someone else You will be in a position to be able to communicate with them even when they are experiencing emotional turmoil.

If you can combine your emotional intelligence with the ability to recognize the subtleties of what someone is communicating, you'll be able to discern the key messages more effectively. This will result in you resolving the situation correctly and making more well-informed decisions. This is because, when you begin to notice more than you can see at a glance and you are able to assess the situation and the person in front of you at a deeper level.

To help you take your understanding of the body language you can read up a notch the next chapter will concentrate on the ability to read gestures, hand gestures and leg movement.

How do you recognize the non-verbal signals of the character of your counterpart

As I began as a coach, I had been educated in the art of strategic and unpersonal communication. However, I soon realized that it wasn't logical to speak only to your student's boss and not speak with the instructor who cuts you out of the class. I believed it would be a slightly more direct and intuitive to address all of them in a certain manner and to set the same expectations of every person, but my clients always came to me with variations of the same query. How do I approach all of them in this manner?

It is not necessary to change our behavior to be more mindful of others. The only thing we have to do is understand the non-verbal messages we get from others to comprehend what they think of us. When we start to "read" one another and begin to understand each other, we will change from being in the hands of other people to being the masters of our own lives.

Learn how to "read" and "understand" other people:

1. Do they behave like you?

Consider for a moment about the message that you will be transmitted by your conduct. Are you friendly? Or passive-aggressive? Does your manner of speaking convey trust or anxiety? Does it appear that you have time for other people as well as time for yourself?

When we meet with people when we meet people, we need to look at how they behave to decide what we need to do and the only option is to behave like us in the way we are perceived or treated by other people. "The first thing to do in diplomatic manner, is to be mindful. If you're treated with respect and respected, you're able to be yourself. If you're being mistreated it is important to be aware," says journalist Ishaan Tharoor.

2. Would they rather a particular type of communication?

In the case of interact with others in a particular way, we are able to identify specific "domains" that we can talk about, such as local celebrities, sports fashion, politics and many more. Within these categories, we have to become adept at operating within these domains. People who look an a particular way in specific domains are more likely to interact with others in this manner, so it is reasonable to assume that they're treating you in exactly the same way.

However those who perform in a specific manner expect you to behave in a specific manner. Therefore, they will react with you in a specific manner. But nobody wants to be treated as an object. And we aren't always able to understand what someone is saying through the way they speak to us. When trying to decide what you should say, consider the manner in which they're addressing you. Are they using facial expressions, body language or hand signals?

3. Do they talk with a flurry of energy?

Eleanor Roosevelt once said, "Nobody can make you feel inferior, without your permission."

This is especially the case in personal and professional relations, as our intuitions could lead us down risky paths, like receiving emails that have been copied and pasted from prior conversations, and expecting other people to recall every single detail of what you discussed the last time, or assuming that everyone is keen on your latest endeavor without considering if they have something else urgently on their minds.

4. Do they feel emotional?

"Emotion is a powerful factor in communicating. It's not because our emotions are harmful but we are susceptible to being manipulated by emotions," explains May Lindley Professor of Psychology in the University of Arizona. When people are angry or shocked, it's usually an indication that they don't enjoy us, or that they're dissatisfied with us, or perhaps that we've done something wrong. If we see that others are angry or angry about us, we need to be ready to read through the conversations.

"Whenever we are angry at someone, we should be aware that they're likely to be angry at the other person," says Lindley.

"We aren't able to comprehend the thoughts of other people and therefore we must be able to converse with someone else in their language rather than the one we speak," says professor Mark Leary from Duke University's Fuqua School of Business.

5. Are they more friendly in person?

A sociologist, author and Kelly Bulkeley said,

"People who make use of the Internet to connect most often are alone and socially isolated while those who are online at the lowest are actively socially."

It is because people prefer to be anonymous and online yet still interact with people in real life. It is more likely for us to feel comfortable in person as opposed to online. When we communicate with someone via email or social media or text, consider how they behave in real life. Do they behave like a friend? Or do they behave as if they're presenting an official presentation?

6. Are they actually truly listening?

If someone is listening to what you are saying and you're listening, you stand a likely possibility of having a productive conversation even if you've not been given the chance to speak. But if someone seems distracted or doesn't appear to be interested in the things you're saying it is likely that you won't receive a positive response from them.

"A successful conversation relies on the listener's ability to ignore you and become autopilot, which means they will not be focused on any topic that isn't relevant," says Ruth Kligman, Ph.D. from Princeton University. "For listeners to achieve this, they must be fully involved, not just with your words, but as well with their own. If they're not, they could be wasting time."

7. Are they becoming defensive?

If you're not getting what that you're looking for, you may be able to anticipate an answer that is similar to this. The thinking process behind this kind of defensive response is typically, "I'm going to point the issue and then make it appear like the issue is not just on me."

8. Do they express your anger on you?

If someone is unhappy, or upset and frustrated, they could be enticed to attack you in a way is beyond your manage. For instance, if you make a witty comment regarding someone's family, and complain of traffic congestion, you could be tempted to say, "Why are you always moaning and complaining?" This type of comment can make it appear like you're making them feel uncomfortable and making them angry. It's a way to make your encounter seem hostile.

"When you see someone angry the first thing you'll want to respond to that frustration," says Lindley. "Try not to be rude when someone is upset. Instead, let your emotions be known and then move to the next step. You'll likely succeed in this kind of circumstance if you stay at peace."

9. Do they call you by name?

The answer, according to Gail Swenson, Ed.D. who was a former psychology instructor in the University of California, San Diego is among the most frequently asked. "If you're communicating with you, or receiving a call or message and doesn't have any idea who you're, they may call your name. If you've ever been in a conference call, you've heard the names of others on the speakerphone, but never your own."

In this case it is your desire for the person who is in front of you to walk up to you and introduce themselves to.

10. Does the person appear to have an expression of envy at their gaze?

Or do they display the look of displeasure? The question, according to Lindley is frequently requested by couples. If you are a guy who is interested in you, he could think you're doing something to get his attention, however actually, you're doing what you're able to do. When a lady is in a relationship with one of her partners and believes you're more attractive than she is and thinks she's losing you that's the kind of look she might give you. If you respond to this question , and the answer is negative, the person you are talking to will likely respond negatively.

11. Are they pulling away from the person?

If you notice the signs of this kind of behavior, it's a good warning signal. "In an instance when you're speaking to people, it's normal to build relationships," says Lindley. "So when someone is acting cold is a sign that they're moving away."

12. Do they show body language that clearly evidence of sarcasm?

"If you're feeling like you're with someone the first thing to make sure to do is greet one others," says Lindley. "When smiling, you're creating eye contact and it generally indicates an that you are open. Don't make the assumption that someone else is angry with you. It's a mistake to make."

13. Do they enjoy your jokes?

"Sarcasm can be subtle and often people get caught up in sarcasm, they don't even realize that they're playing jokes," says Lindley. "If you're telling a joke it's a sign that the person you are talking to is friendly and you shouldn't be scared to make fun of the jokes they make."

14. Do they appear at all bored?

It's probably the top concern people ask. You may be in the middle of a conversation however If the person you're talking to is apathetic is a sign they're not truly fully engaged. They might not pay any attention to what you're saying.

There are people who use the phone to make calls for convenience, claims Kligman. "In these instances people don't even know that they're doing it," says Kligman. "If you're talking over the phone and then the person stands up and leaves their room, it might be giving you a subtle signal that they're just not interested."

15. Do they cut off your communication?

The abrupt and abrupt manner of speaking is another sign to watch out for. "You're on a date and someone interrupts you , and you aren't able to comprehend the words they're using," says Lindley. "That's an important warning signal. If you do this on the night of a date, they do not care about you, and may call you in the future."

One sign that someone blocking you might not be really interested in you, according to Lindley If they don't answer your texts or calls. "If you find someone rude and doesn't answer your messages or calls then you can be sure they're not going to return your calls," says Lindley. "You could take this as a warning."

16. Does the person who is giving an answer that is only one word?

When you're with such as "So how do you do at work?" isn't difficult. "If they reply with only one word, it's an extremely good indication that you shouldn't be with you," says Lindley.

One word answers means they could not even have a job and could be bored of the questions you ask.

17. Are they observing other individuals?

"Asking people about what their job is for an income is a great question to ask. However, If they're not paying attention, and are wandering around instead of looking at you they're not really engaged in conversation with you." tells Lindley. "They could be looking at the room or could use you as an excuse to stop for a moment."

19. Do they alter the subject each time you mention something they do not agree with?
"Someone who isn't a fan of you will do everything to stop you from speaking to them," says Lindley. "When you talk about something they do not like the person will cease listening. If you pose a question they consider controversial, they'll get angry about you."

This could be due to the fact that the person

you're with does not have enough knowledge of you however it's something you should be aware of in determining whether or not the relationship is going to go well.

20. Do they react differently depending on the person?

Another indication to avoid dating the person you're talking to, according to Lindley. "When you tell someone"Hey, I saw this cool person at work the other night and they were really cool,'" Lindley says. Lindley. "They'll probably be interested in meeting with the person However, should you inform them of the same thing, they'll most likely shift the topic. They may have no interest in the personand might not be eager to get to know that person."

Chapter 6: All About Mirroring

Mirroring is a visual method of communication in which one person during the interaction subconsciously mirrors or imitates the posture, the verbal pattern or gestures of another. It is most common in social situations, especially when with close family or close friends. The notion usually connects individuals' views on the person who has been displaying the mirroring behavior and could result in the mirroring person forming a connection with the other person.

If nonverbal signals are reproduced in a subconscious manner by another individual and are reflected back to them, this is referred to as "mirroring." Mirroring is present in all communication that occurs all day long, and typically is not noticed by the people who are mirroring, and the person who mirrors. Mirroring neurons get activated in the individual who starts to mirror the actions of another individual which allows them to have to have a greater connection and understanding of the person who is mirroring, in addition to mirroring allows the person being mirrored to perceive more closely the person who is being mirrored. Mirroring is different from copying that is acutely aware in the sense that the former is extremely aware. In general, when people express the desire to duplicate another person's actions, the subconscious act of mirroring occurs throughout the interaction , but usually gets ignored.

The mirroring show generally begins when the baby is born. Mirroring the people around them, they form relations through the expression of the body. The capacity to mimic the actions of a person lets the child see the ways of everyday sensations and thus begins to understand the emotions of another. The child can discover connections between completely different emotions in people and at when they are able to mimic the actions of others.

Mirroring creates a connection to the person mirrored because the similarity in nonverbal gestures permit individuals to feel connected to the person who is displaying the behavior that is reflected. When the two individuals in the same situation display the same gestures, which are similar and nonverbal, a person is able to feel that they share common concepts and actions. Mirror neurons react to gestures and trigger the actions happen, allowing the participants to feel a greater engagement sensation and feeling of joy within their own.

Mirroring usually doesn't occur at all levels of conscious awareness when people are engaged in diverse circumstances. Mirroring occurs in speech due to the fact that people who are listening to the speech can smile and frown when they hear someone speaking, and also mimicking the angle, posture or body posture of the speaker with respect to the topic. It is also possible that people are inclined to empathize with and accept people whom they share opinions and interests, thus mirroring the speaker can result in connections among the individuals involved.

Interviews

Additionally, mirroring may play a role in the way the individual is in an interaction. For instance, Word, Zanna, and Cooper conducted interviews in which participants were instructed to follow certain types of visual communication throughout a variety of situations during the experiment. In one particular scenario participants conducting the interview were required to communicate an uninterested, distant visual communication, like refusing to make eye contact or physically move away. In another situation, they were required to display friendly visual language, such as smiling and engaging their eyes. As a result of their circumstances they began mirroring the behavior of the interviewer and the individuals in the interview who had distant or less "friendly" visually communicated performed better in interviewing than people in the scenario that were "friendlier." Its findings show that the initial behavior that the interviewer might exhibit towards the interviewee could affect the response due to mirroring.

The consequences of poor mirroring skills

People who have disabilities or social challenges could also be restricted in their capacity to exhibit mirroring abilities, since they may not be consciously or unconsciously receptive to the actions of others. This can cause additional problems for people because if they don't mirror the other person, building relationships with them might be difficult. Additionally, other individuals may struggle to form an emotional connection with the person in the absence of mirroring, since the person could be unlikable to them and therefore not so likable.

People who don't appear to be consciously sensitive to the expression of their thoughts should face issues in public speaking because they will not be able to discern an alternative viewpoint when it's no longer formally spoken, and therefore might not be conscious of subtle clues that are commonly used in public places. It's possible, but terribly difficult for a handful of them to deliberately study and be open to clues. However, this isn't the norm; it's an rare exception. This isn't the norm.

Development

When parents are engaged in parental duties, mirroring is the process of the parent or father mirroring the child's behavior including music that reflects the emotion expressed through the actions. Mirroring helps children to associate the feelings with their behavior similarly as a way to confirm the thoughts of their own, since the father or mother show acceptance through imitation. Studies have shown that imitation is an essential aspect of infant and toddler development. Based on the theory of self-psychology proposed by Kohut Human beings select ways to express their acceptance and happiness in order to define their own thoughts about their own self. If people and women emulate their child, the imitation should aid in the growth into a higher level of control and attention to self-control, since the child will be able to be able to observe their emotions taking place in the faces that their caregivers. Additionally, children may wish to study and understand new emotions as well as expressions on their face and their actions by imitating the actions of their parents. Imitating their parents' behavior will give babies the ability to build relationships between actions and thoughts , and thus enable social conversations when they develop. Children also seek to be that they are in a way inaccessible and valid in their own thoughts by mirroring. This is because the reflection of their parents of their emotions should help the child to recognize their own thoughts and feelings.

Self-concept

Mirroring has been shown to be an essential element in the development of a baby's understanding about themselves. Mirroring is a crucial aspect of development. that babies acquire their social skills from their caregivers, therefore a social group which is unable to mirror could hinder the child's growth in social situations. If there is no mirroring then it's difficult for the child to express their emotions through the world and encounter difficult situations in which they have to sharing of their emotions.

Empathy

Inability to properly reflect particular people can affect the child's relationships throughout their lives. This stress could come in the form of others , and may cause parents or fathers being unable to communicate with the infant due to an absence of contact or as a result that the child is not mirroring or observing an unpleasant experience of feeling connected to other people. Mirroring helps in fostering a feelings of commonality, and can help in expressing particular people's emotions are replicated through imitation of the movements and postures of others. This recurring feeling should help humans build lasting bonds and increase social bonds. Mirroring is a method of letting people believe that they are perfectly suited or exactly the same with other people and the commonality seen as the basis to create connections. Mirroring therefore is essential and significant.

Rapport

Rapport should also be an integral aspect of our social lives, since developing rapport with someone is generally the most effective way to make close relationships or being a part of anyone else. Mirroring can help establish relationships, since displaying similar behavior, expressions and speech patterns as any other person can help them to think that someone is exactly like their own and therefore makes the impression of being an all-around friend. One should believe that the result of mirroring the gestures of another, they will have similar values and beliefs as a mirror of their own. Mirroring could also be engaged in intimate relationships or romantic relationships, since the individuals consider each other extremely high, and thus tend to emulate or even pacify their counterparts. Additionally, those who are friends with one another might want to be able to connect with two people who haven't had a conversation, and thus might be capable of showing similar visual communication, despite mirroring.

Power Dynamics

Additionally to that, individuals have the potential to mirror those with a higher status or influence within social contexts. Mirroring those with more influence can create an image of a higher status or create relationships with the person or person with influence, which allows individuals to be favored to the person with influence. It could benefit humans in any situation where people interact with an individual who has more power, since the reflections created by mirroring are likely be able to help the person with more influence in order to help the person of lesser influence. This includes interviews for jobs, specific situations at work such as asking for a promotion, conversations between parents and children or soliciting the help of an instructor.

Every single one of those aspects has a particular participant with greater fame and has a high level of influence and a different participant with the capacity to meet the demands of the person or woman who has less influence they may not opt to. This is why mirroring is an ideal tool for those with low reputation to influence other participants, causing them to sacrifice their skills or capabilities for the less reputation participant.

What is Mirrored Body Language Four Strategies for Remarkably Mirroring Others

Reflecting on others can be amusing. Anyone who has had to deal with someone who repeats everything you do and say will be a victim of this. However, this could change from being enjoyable to irritating quickly.

"Pretend to be someone else, and take a break from pretending" When you're done your body is "fronting" the person and making eye contact and using that "triple gesture." You have created a profound impression and strong connection but, to prove it, use your imagination's abilities. Try this technique using "pretending" to appear to be the person you're with is the most captivating, attractive person you've met in your lifetime. Imagine it's real and then respond to this belief. Then, finally, you can stop "pretending."

Through all these actions Mirroring can be seen most likely occurring in a natural way, there are some mirroring techniques that can be utilized to improve their connection to you.

2. Volume and pace
Most people think of mirroring as reflecting the actions of their body. or in relation to any non-verbal communication. Start by using mirrors to reflect the level and pace of the other person's speech. If they're a fantastic fast speaker, booming then increase the speed and the volume that you speak. If the other person is quiet, slow, and relaxed rather reflect their voice at this point. Making sure that the volume and the pace match is easy to accomplish and is less obvious than mimicking physical movements

3. Find the other's "Punctuator"
If you've been attentively watching the person watching the whole conversation and you might have noticed a favorite "punctuator," which the other party relies on to highlight an important point. It could be the brow "flash," which is fast eyebrow lifting or a gesture using their hands, like the ones politicians normally make.

This is an example of how the term "punctuator" is a tool that can be utilized. A person, earlier this year, was having lunch with a physician who was pitching a private personal, as well as an institutional partnership. The person who was meeting with the doctor noticed it was when the physician seemed intense about a matter the doctor would hold each of their hands before their body, and push the hands carefully upwards and downwards. While the doctor spoke, the other person was able to influence the doctor through a nod in unison with his comments and when the medical professional came to an end, the other person mimicked the gesture of the doctor's two hands as it were if the person who was doing the creating it by themselves. The doctor paused, cocked their head and replied, "Yes! You're completely clear!" and smiled with an earful. The peculiarity of the situation is that the person did not have to say a word.

4.Checking the Association
The last option is elective. But, if you would like to examine your link, make an explicit act that isn't related to the subject you're speaking about and see if the behaviour is visible to the other users. After a keynote presentation during a break, the presenter given a speech, a person in the audience walked up to the presenter and spoke about the similarities the audience member and

the presenter in relation to the family story of their own which was told during the presentation. While the presenter was speaking to the speaker, they noticed an uncomfortable itch on their nose, which they swiftly stroked. The person in the audience then raised his or her arm , and rub their noses while telling their story. The incident appeared to be strange and the speaker made the an initiative to examine the mirroring to see whether it was indeed an actual reflection. After a few seconds the speaker was rubbing their head and an spectator suddenly took exactly the same thing. It was evidently an imitation that the speaker was able to test and confirm. But beware, avoid doing recurrent checks since this could quickly break the link!

Last but not least, if you have reflected someone, make sure that you are expressing positively positive behavior and manner of communication and not displaying negative behavior, like the avoidance of interference, crossed arms, closed eyes or a desire to be away.

Now is the time to go out into the world and build links to others. And should you be inclined to mirror your actions correctly it is making two reflections into one.

Chapter 7: Nonverbal Socializing

Social Groups

If we are capable of altering the way others view us Does that mean that we're able to make friends more easily? Humans are social animals and it's important to establish the circle of reliable acquaintances and friends. Anthropologist Robin Dunbar, studied apes while they were in group social settings. He was able to figure out the number of people who were in close proximity to each other for grooming, like grooming friends according to the size of their neocortex brain. Chimps for instance have a circle of friends that is around 50 people, but only have a couple of grooming buddies. Humans have a bigger Neocortex than both chimps and apes. Thus, by extrapolating the findings, he concluded that humans can have an outside social circle that can be as large as 150 individuals. However, just like the Chimps, the number drops for close relationships to approximately 12 people. A different thing about humans is that they communicate through language and bond, unlike chimps, who rely on grooming.

It is clear that our method of communication allows us to create more social networks. There's nothing more embarrassing than having a fake group of friends. They let us down when we're in need. Develop your communication skills to be able to better understand body language. After that, you'll be able to select your friends with care.

Manipulation In The Most Elegant Way

The ability to read nonverbal gestures which reveal an individual's thoughts is an effective instrument. In a way you can alter how others perceive you by using how you move.

If we are drawn to a person we've had the pleasure of meeting, not always in the romantic manner We try at impressing them. To make the right decisions, we must know more about their character. If we pay close at non-verbal signals this gives us an advantage of making the correct decisions.

This is the time that eye contact is crucial. If someone else turns their eyes from yours and then you know they're not in the mood or perhaps they're timid. If you keep using your new skills in communication then you'll be able to dig into the details and figure out the reason.

Utilize your body language to demonstrate that

you don't have anything to cover up. Do not make sudden or unplanned movements. It's wiser to be patient when making moves. Don't fumble or twitch nervously. Be clear so others feel like you're calm and confident. Do not overexaggerate when speaking. talk. Keep your arms in a low position and your movements soft. A calm, controlled manner can help you appear as a person in control.

Keep using the warm smile and switch it throughout the day to appear more friendly. If you can feel the smile, it will make you feel better and will appear warm and welcoming.

It's not just about your body language however. Pay attention to your own phrases, for instance when you are offering the person you're buying drinks, do not appear as if you're offering them favors. Instead try to make it sound like an act of kindness like: "I'm about to order an alcoholic drink and would you like to have one?"

This way you're showing the willingness of you to "share." You're asking them to be part of your. Your body language should be relaxed and you are also open it means that you are creating a comfortable atmosphere in the best way you can. If they're in agreement, that is your signal to move towards your own space. Be cautious as a bit too quickly could turn the relationship to downwards spiral.

If a conversation is going on be sure to pay attention to their words and react to them by expressing your body. Making sure you are pointing your head in the correct places is a good place to start. You're in a position to benefit because you know they'll follow your movement in the background. Move closer to them if you are able to. This shows that you're taking an interest in what they are saying.

Another option can be to mimic their movement however, don't make it obvious. If they tilt their heads you should tilt your head as well. Be careful not to overdo it, there is an important line to walk when to walk when you are getting to walk. Mirroring's importance is evident in a 2008 study (19). In a test with students who were in a negotiation situation, those who mirror performed well in the test 67 percent times. Students who didn't mirror did so only 12.5 percent on average.

When you can feel the connection betweenyou and them, you will be able to see their reflection on your behavior. Try a sigh, since this will always work. Now you have a subject of conversation to talk about, "erm...I think we both did not get enough sleep last night, what's the reason?" As they respond by leaning closer, listen to what they say.

If they are closing up in their posture, like cross-legged or turning over the upper portion of their body, don't reflect. This type of posture isn't nice. You must get the other person to be relaxed. You can show them your vulnerable areas like moving your head back bit and exposing your throat. Take your hands off and expose your palms. When you expose yourself in this manner, you're opening your heart to them.

When you observe and mirror their actions, you're making yourself more in tune and with them. This can help establish a relationship so that you are able to identify with one the other. If you're together, you can conduct the meeting in a similar manner. As you're both evaluating each others, it's you who is leading the direction. It's because you've spent the time to develop an understanding of subtle signals. If you're looking for a relationship to be successful, bring out the best of your self and that person.

Chapter 8: Expressions Of The Face

Consider for a moment how much an individual can communicate with only a glance. A smile could signify the feeling of happiness or approval. A frown could indicate an attitude of disapproval or discontent.

In some cases our facial expressions could be a sign of our true attitudes towards a specific event. If you claim that you're fine however, the way you look at your face may let people know that.

A few examples of feelings that could be expressed by facial expressions are:

* Happiness
* Sadness
* Anger
* Surprise
* Disgust
* Fear
* Confused
* Excited
* Desire
* Contempt

The way someone's eyes look can help determine whether we agree or disagree with what the individual or the female is saying.

A study found that the most honest facial expression was a slight raising of the eyebrows, and an unintentionally smile. The expression, as the researchers suggested, communicates confidence and friendliness.

Face expressions are also some of the most well-known types of body expressions. Expressions that convey emotion such as sadness, anger and joy are similar all over the world.

A researcher has found a solution to the universality of a wide range of facial expressions linked to specific emotions like emotion, anger as well as fear, shock and sadness.

Research suggests that we judge the intelligence of people primarily on their appearance and facial expressions.

One study revealed that those with smaller faces and noses with more distinct features are better seen as being intelligent. People who have happy, smiling faces have also been deemed to be more intelligent than those with angry faces.

Chapter 9: How The Legs Show What The Minds Wants To Do

The legs and feet which are often ignored when studying body language, convey lots of important information about what we're experiencing, thinking about and experiencing. We pay such focus on our face , and the other parts of the body that we do not realize the importance of these important parts of our bodies.

It's a mistake that a lot of us make, and should not, as in many ways, the legs and feet are the most precise part of our bodies. They reveal our true feelings and intentions in real-time, unlike our face and other areas of our bodies.

Furthermore, they are a key element in detecting deceit.

Through the ages our limbic system was able to make sure that our legs and feet were ready to react immediately in the face of any danger or issue Their reliability has ensured at least a portion of our survival. Someone approaches us at night, while we're in front of the ATM machine, and our legs begin to tighten and our feet turn toward an escape route and we are ready to escape should we need to.

Similar to this our limbic brain warns our feet to not move far enough from the top edge. So we do not. When we are crossing our legs, we are at ease in the elevator, however, when a group of untrustworthy strangers arrive, we swiftly cross our legs to ensure that we can get away in the event of need. We're talking to one of our friends and then we see that one of their feet is pointed towards the street. It's not necessary to ask you, they must go and are over time to an appointment. Are you curious to find out if there are two people in the hallway are like you or want to be a part of them? If their feet aren't moving to greet you, and they only move their hips, they'll just continue walking along. If the relationship is beginning to turn to a negative direction, you will see more and less contact between feet. The couple may be able to touch in public but their feet stay away from each other.

They are limbic responses which are expressed in the legs and feet, to events, feelings and even intentions. They are extremely timely and precise. In the same way, a child could be eating at a table however, if he decides to go outside and play take note of the way his feet move, as they extend to the floor from the high chair even though he's not yet eaten his food. Try to keep him in place however, he'll wiggle in a way, and then his feet pivot towards the closest exit, which is a precise reflection that his foot is where are located and where want to take him. This is a signal to indicate intent and we have many which we can use to express our desire to accomplish something.

Since our legs and feet are so truthful I put a lot of emphasis on the way they express themselves while looking for signs of deceit. The majority of people concentrate on the face, however the face is excellent at deceiving. As young as we are, we are taught "don't put on that face," regardless of how much we are not happy with the way we are taught. As we grow older, the practice is not over, and we continue to put on the "party face" to please our spouse or smile because the society we're from demands it. So we pretend to be our feelings or thoughts by putting on our faces (thus creating a "poker appearance") to maintain peace and harmony in the social realm. It is also a way to avoid being caught doing something dishonest. Our legs and feet as they are essential to survive, should not make any concessions to this.

In My book "What Everybody Is Saying "Nervousness and stress anxiety, fear boredom, restlessness joy, sadness timidity, coyness confidence, humility, awkwardness subservience, depression insanity, lethargy and anger are all able to manifest in the legs and feet." While I conducted interviews for the FBI I mainly was focused on the legs and feet precisely because they provide many details about what's going on inside the mind. Lie-tellers are aware of their facial displays however not so much about their feet or feet.

Over the course of 25 years, I have observed and recording behavior for the FBI I observed that when people start in a lie, they usually disengage themselves by standing farther than you. or, they put at you with their feet however they turn toward your body by bending their body. This appears normal on first examination, but these are distancing movements that provide a good idea of the state of their brain.

People who lie tend to not emphasize. They know what they want to say, but they don't know the feelings that accompany the words they use We see less gravitas-defying actions when they are speaking. True people are known be defying gravity with standing over their feet while insisting on a point or raising their eyebrows. Falsehoods do not because gravity defying behavior are limbically derived, emotional expressions expressed through body language, something they do not have.

If we're honest our feet will be more robust and wider in position. When we are feeling uneasy regarding the words we use or if we lie our feet will be a bit closer. It's an emotional response that is tied to the way we feel (insecure) about what's being said. If we don't feel confident in our thoughts it shows in our feet and legs.

If a person is lying the deceiver is anxious about being caught and what you can be able to observe is that fear sometimes is the reason for what I have called"the "Ankle Quiver." This is when the ankle starts to twitch , causing the individual to rock their foot sideways , back and forth (bottom side to the edge of the foot). The truthful person does not have reason to feel smug through this repetitive rocking However, a lying person could consider these "under the table" behavior that are self-soothing.

And lastly, and these are clearly not the only actions of the foot and leg to be observed, you should look out at the person who announces their intentions before performing the leg wash. In the act of rubbing his hands (sometimes several times) across the tops of his legs, while sitting and seated, it calms the person who is deceiving or has guilt. This usually happens when explicit, serious questions are asked. This can lead to an extreme amount of discomfort.

To gain more understanding of the role of feet and legs in looking for deceit chapter three of What Everyone is Saying describes more precisely how we can utilize the legs and feet to discern human behaviour. When you are pondering the behavior of other people to discover what they're thinking or feeling or intending to think be aware that feet and legs are crucial in this search because they do not fall short in their precision.

Chapter 10: Power Of Hands Power Of Hands

The hands are a source of power that we don't even know about, so we do not pay attention to the power of hands. They transmit a vast amount of messages that the majority of people are unable to comprehend.

Hands are used for centuries in conversations but their significance has changed many times over time. A good example is a handshake.

Handshakes is rooted in the earlier times. When ancient tribes gathered they would shake their palms to demonstrate they were not concealing anything.

The Roman Empire utilized to tighten the wrists of the forearms, to ensure they did not conceal anything beneath his sleeves. This was done due to the fact that at the time, it was commonplace to go about using a knife beneath the sleeve , and it was considered safe. The custom was adopted by the time.

However, like the other traditions passed down from generation to generation this one, which was popular among the Romans has evolved into our handshake.

This gesture is utilized in a variety of different scenarios. The gestures ranged from the traditional greeting of acquaintances to handshakes to create a formal agreement between two multinational corporations.

Even in Japan where the traditional greeting was always with a bow, the gesture of handshake has become often used.

The fact that it's widely used doesn't mean it's easy to perform. Behind the handshake is a world of dominance and submission.

In the past, in Rome two people would greet one another by hand-wrestling I'll will define it as a handshake.

It was not commonplace to shake hands like we do now, but one person grabbed the other's hand from top to bottom and formed the appearance of a sandwich so to say. The strongest person was able to dominate the other.

Today, this method isn't used anymore, but the person you choose to win is present when you handshake. There are three types of handshakes that can be concluded that are:

* Dominance
* Submit
* Equality

The way we perceive these attitudes is in the subconscious and the body processes these in a specific manner, and each of them will decide the direction that conversation should be.

One example I could give you is from the study conducted on a few executives of companies. Male or female makes no difference.

It's been proven that 89% people use the dominant handshake. They should always put their hands out first, so they can hold their hand in a precise manner.

It is the exact opposite of the submissive handshake. In this scenario the person shakes his palms up and gives the other supremacy. Similar to what dogs do when they lie down , they lay their bodies to the sky.

It is a good idea to use this handshake to make your friend to feel at ease with the situation. It is possible to use this technique when you want to justify your actions for instance.

However in the event that two individuals are in a situation which they both desire to turn over the other's side to gain control the other, there is a "bite" occurs. This leads to the two people to be equally matched, and neither, at the end of the day, will be the upper hand.

If you're looking to build a rapport with the

person who is in the front of you, keep his hand turning however, you must apply the same amount of force the person is using.

Let's look at the hypothetical numbers. If you apply the force that is 9 out of 10 to the handshake, and you apply a force of 7 from 10, you'll be required to increase the force or else you'll be controlled. Similar thing that you need to perform reversed if you do not intend to win.

In other words the simplest way, if he uses 5 force and you apply a force of 7, If you don't want to appear dominant, you'll have to reduce the force of your grip.

Now, I'll share how to not allow yourself to be controlled. Even if you had to meet with the president of the United States.

With this strategy you will always, and, I repeat always be ahead of your opponent. If you're looking to win, do it.

The method is known as "disarming the perpetrators."

The procedure involves placing your arm outstretched, and the palm facing downwards so that you do not open any doors for your opponent who will then have to move his hand to hold it in submission.

From then onwards, you're free to do what you

like. You can decide to be dominant or share the same position, however, it's extremely difficult for him make the situation work in his favor. Similar to what happens in games where you are three points ahead of your opponent and the game is set to end, the player has to make a miraculous play to win. In reality the only options available to him are to draw or lose.

If you encounter a situation of someone holding his hand out, in the manner described above, there's a way you can do in order to rectify the situation.

Move forward using your left foot, and make sure that you bring your hand in a vertical direction. This exercise is not easy since we usually move to the right however, you'll see that it is much more naturally for you after some practice.

If you're not able to do this There is a second option to keep yourself from dominance which is to take advantage of the double-catch.

When your partner hands you up then you take your other hand to turn the hold back into tie. Now you're using two hands , whereas you are using one hand.

Being Left-leaning is an unfair advantage

In a handshake, your positioning is important and staying to the left side is helpful when you are trying to be dominant.

This happens because on the right hand side, you are not in control of the situation. On the left, you are able to actually take control of it.

Kennedy loved this method very greatly, even though, at the time, little was available about body language. Kennedy was already using it via instinct.

If you look through every photo of him meeting with famous and powerful people and leaders, you'll always see him to the left, with his double grip.

One of the most striking examples that shows what Kennedy was a sensation with body language was when he was a winner in Nixon. Nixon election.

In the era of Nixon, it was said that those who had only heard the speeches of two politicians believed that Nixon had prevailed, while people who watched the event were not convinced.

It helped Kennedy to be the winner of his presidential election. This body language is pretty crucial does it not?

But, referring back to the previous speech and assuming you're in the middle of the image to be in the same circumstance, you can reach out and get him to shake his hand in the manner you'd like.

To wrap up, I offer you the summary.

Many people don't realize the impression they can leave to a stranger even though they're aware of how important it is to provide an excellent starting point for the course of a conversation.

Try experimenting using various handshakes possibly family, friends or colleagues at work to become familiar with the process. In important situations, you will know the right way to behave.

Chapter 11: The Secret Handshake

In the modern world that we live in, you might believe that it's what you wear, the car you drive, and the place you work that leads the public to develop opinions on your character. However, that's not entirely the situation.

Experts believe it takes about four minutes to form a basic perception of someone. Four minutes. In that amount of time, unless they're trying to impress you, you will not know the location they reside in or what vehicle they drive or maybe the things they work for money.

The factors you're going to base your opinion on could be things that you do not be aware of. Little physical items.

Eye contact, where they're standing, the way they shake hands.

This is because how you shake hands with someone..., or the way you shake hands with someone else... can be one of the primary factors in how we form opinions about each others.

To keep this thought in mind Let's look at hand shaking and discover the meaning behind your handshake. you.

Where did the handshake originate from?

If you're contemplating shaking hands, it is an odd thing to perform in our daily lives. When you meet an individual in the very first place, after you conclude an important business meeting or ending an official gathering and you greet them with a handshake.

The most nerve-wracking handshake you can offer when meeting one on the first date.

The tradition originates from the ancient city of Rome. When a battle was over, and an victory, Generals were expected to greet one their counterparts with a clapping of hands. They would do something a bit different from what the way we greet each other today and stood closer and raise their arms in a higher position.

One reason they'd do this is to decide who was

the first to take the cut of the bounty. Whoever was the general with his hands on the top even if only slight, would take the first shot at the bounty and wine.

This is where our phrase "having an upper hand" originates.

What does your handshake say about you

If two generals were to hold hands and the grip was identical to both men, they'd split their celebrations and spoils in the middle and start simultaneously. If this were the case the generals would each try to replicate the grip of the other.

With this in mind Let's take it back to here and here and now. Do you have a great handshake? What message does your handshake send to the world?

To begin, we often shake hands in a way that isn't correct. Men appear too powerful and forceful as a way of daily life, while women are more likely to give hands that are limp. This is usually a result of the norm, but it's something that you can overcome regardless of the actions you take.

The reason I'm concerned about the quality of your handshake is that it helps to assist those who meet you make a judgement about your character.

A handshake that is too forceful

It is likely that the moment you get to know someone you should offer them a firm, nice hand. This is certainly true to some extent. It is important to provide them a firm grip, however, you shouldn't overdo it.

A handshake that's too powerful will seem intimidating and could be a source of fear for those you have just had a conversation with. Although you might think that it's a good idea initially, you should consider that you do not want to be intimidating to your prospective employer, or someone you're trying to invite out for an evening date.

Try to be strong, but not overly strong.

The noodle is limp

As I mentioned that women are more likely to give an unintentionally weak handshake more often than males and this is usually non-intentional. They do it due to being nervous or intimidated by the circumstance or are trying to look feminine.

There's nothing wrong in being feminine, however, it's not a good idea to let that show through when you shake hands. This is because we're conditioned to know who has the upper hand when we meet people first for the first time and if you're offering an arm that is limp the person you're meeting will conclude that you'll perform anything they'd like to do.

This isn't to say that they're going to be thinking that way or asking for it However, it's the overall impression they have, and that's the thing I would like to know about. You'll want to demonstrate you're feminine however, you should be able to stand you own within the event.

Just right

The perfect handshake also known as the handshake that's just right is one that is equally to both hands. Equal pressure is used equally in the handshake and done for the same length of time.

Everyone has an edge since they are both identical. When you meet at the center, and you both show that you've got the same power behind your movements, and then you let go simultaneously.

It's a simple concept in principle, but stunning when it's executed but it requires learn to.

How to create the perfect handshake

When someone tries to do the perfect handshake right from the beginning, they are likely to be overly strong. Women are particularly likely to overcompensate and will end up squeezing way too forcefully and pumping their hands as if they are operating an old-fashioned mining cart.

Men are more likely to do the opposite when it comes to pressure, and even if they are trying to ease the pressure they don't apply much pressure, creating the impression that they're not sure.

But, there's hope. It is possible to master the perfect handshake. It only takes a bit of practice to master it.

Step 1.

The first thing you should do when you're going in for an exchange of hands is to hold your hand in a straight position. Place your hands directly in front of you with your thumb up and your pinky on the bottom.

When you do this , that your hand naturally sways in one direction or another. It may not be so any significant amount, and you need to be looking to determine how your hand tips however I can assure you that it will.

Practice straightening it , and extend it in this straight way. This is likely require some practice because you might exaggerate in one direction or another. It is important to grasp straight with your hands perfectly straight.

Once you've mastered this then you're prepared to move to the next step.

Step 2.

After your hand is in contact with the other's hand It is easy to gauge the amount of pressure they're applying and try to be in line with the same amount of pressure. If the handshake is executed perfect, both hold their hands upright with palms firmly together. exactly the same pressure level is applied to both sides.

Both parties will feel comfortable about the interaction and neither of them will feel intimidated or superior.

Step 3.

When your hands meet the palms, put equal force to both sides and take a look at one another in the eyes. You'll be able to see that something changes as you perform this.

If you both look at each one in the eyes while applying the same pressure to each other, your handshake will be natural and you'll be pumping at the same rate and for the same duration of time.

If something isn't quite right However, the handshake will be a bit off. If the person you're with refuses to look you in the eyes or even just glances at you at you for a moment before looking away, they're going immediately give an impression that they're not sure of themselves. You are likely to grab the hand of theirs a bit more. It is important to keep this in check and to practice keeping that same amount of pressure in your hand regardless of what they do.

Also, if your handshakes are well-matched the two of you will engage for the same length of time. However, should the other person look away, they will not initiate any handshakes, and you're forced to handle the whole thing on your own.

Do not stand and shake and shake their hands. A couple of up down motions are enough to release your hand and continue ahead with the conversation. Although you might be able to hold your handshake, it will still appear to be a victim of nervousness if you hold your hand over for too long.

Do people really think about their hands this so

much?

It's not that conscious, and people don't put that much of time and effort in shaking hands, yet subconsciously we are unable to resist it. As we're constantly analysing the actions of those that surrounds us, so we look at the finer details of our lives without even realizing that we are.

You judge your actions according to your own assessment and other people base their decisions on that foundation and only when they perform the same thing and they're analyzing you.

Chapter 12: Touch

We often touch. We often shake hands to express greetings or to indicate that we are in agreement. Touch as a means of communication is known as haptics. Touch is for children an essential aspect of their development. Children who do not receive enough touch may have issues with their development. Touch can help infants cope with stress. When they are infants it is the first sensory experience that infants respond to.

Functional Touch

In the workplace, touch can be a powerful method of communication, however it is essential to maintain a professional tone or informal. Handshakes, for instance, are usually exchanged in the professional setting and be a sign of trust between two individuals. Be aware of the non-verbal signals that you're conveying the when you shake hands with someone. All in all, it is important to be confident when shaking the other person's hand , but not be overly confident. The words of praise and encouragement are usually conveyed through gentle pats in the back. Be aware that people have different responses to touch when it comes to nonverbal communications. For instance, a harmless touch may make another feel uncomfortable or fearful. Touch can be a challenge when it is between the boss and subordinate. Most of the time, people in charge use contact with subordinates to strengthen the structure in the office. It's not a good idea for this to happen in the reverse direction. Therefore, it is important to be vigilant even when applying the smallest of touch and then resolve to enhance your methods of communication with your kids. The most common rule is to make mistakes but stay cautious. Functional touch is when you are medically examined by a doctor and being touched to perform a type of professional massage.

Social Touch

The United States, a handshake is the most popular way to show affection in social interactions. Handshakes differ between cultures, however. In certain countries where kissing both or one cheeks is more popular than handshakes. Similar to the interactions, males will let male acquaintances kiss them on their shoulders or arms, while women prefer being approached by female strangers only on their arms. Men will likely enjoy touching from female strangers and women feel uncomfortable when touched from strangers of males. Also both genders respond to touch differently, which could cause awkward and uncomfortable situations. It is important to be respectful and careful. If, for instance, you're standing near an individual in an elevator, it's unacceptable to be close enough to them that you touch them.

Friendship Touch

The kind of touching that is permitted between friends can differ depending on the setting. For instance, females are more open to touching female acquaintances than male friends. The way that people interact with each other is based on the proximity of the family as well as gender that the member of your family. The gestures of affection between family members are usually welcomed and are necessary even if you're not one of them. It is important to step out the comfort zones and give your friend a hug when they are struggling. The act of helping others boost their moods will likely boost your mood too.

Intimacy Touch

For romantic partnerships, gestures that show affection play a crucial part. For instance, even the most basic of gestures can convey the message of love, for instance handshakes or placing your arms around your partner to signal that you're together. Adults tend to focus more on non-verbal cues than communication via verbal signals in recent research regarding communication. In the early stages of dating, guys are more likely to initiate physical contact according to the norms of society, however in later phases the women are the ones who make contact. Women put more emphasis on contact than men, and even the smallest gestures can calm women who are upset with.

Arousal Touch

Arousing touch triggers emotions that are intense and only permissible if they are they are mutually agreed upon. Arousal gestures are designed to create a sense of pleasure. They can be characterized by hugging, kissing or flirtatious touches and are usually meant to suggest sex. It is important to be aware of the needs of their partner. It is possible to greatly enhance your interpersonal skills and relationships by taking note of the nonverbal messages you communicate through touching behaviors.

In addition our sensation of touch is designed to convey information clearly and swiftly. Touch can elicit subconscious communication. For example, you immediately withdraw your fingers when you touch something that is hot, but before you think about processing. This is why touch is among the most efficient ways of communicating. Touch as a method of non-verbal communicating is an automatic type of communication. In particular, it transmits information in a flash and triggers an immediate guttural response. If you do not touch it, it sends false messages to you without awareness.

Methods to Improve Touch in appropriate contexts

Give someone a pat on the back whenever you show them appreciation.

If a friend or colleague has been promoted, graduated, promotion, or got married, then you should give them a pat on the back. A pat on the back indicates that you're happy with the person and helping them. The therapeutic benefits of touch are that calms the mind and the body while making a person feel safe and valued. In school, you should have felt loved and valued by those who brushed you by the teacher.

Begin discussions by introducing a touch to build connections.

The results of studies have shown that touching an individual improves their ability to collaborate and to work with other people. Making contact with the person you want to have a conversation with will help. In some cases, the person you are trying to contact may not even realize the touch, but will sense the touch and create an emotional connection.

Make sure to extend the handshakes.

Handshakes show confidence and ease in communicating with other people. Handshakes help to build trust between two people. Try to be solid when you shake hands with others. It is also important to keep in mind that certain illnesses can make someone avoid shaking hands. This can be caused by hyperhidrosis which causes hands of people sweat. If the hands are sweaty one is more likely to avoid handshakes, and this has nothing to do with have to do with the nature of the conversation.

Change the type of touch in relation to the context.

As mentioned, touch is extremely congruous. For example it is the case that the Japanese don't like shaking hands, and anyone who lives in Japan will be careful about the act of shaking hands at any cost. In the American environment shake hands are accepted. To avoid this, you should alter your touch style based on the situation. It may be acceptable to touch your companion for a long time, but the opposite is very creepy when speaking to strangers or a coworker at work.

A different form of contact is tickling. It is generally reserved for loved ones, parents as opposed to children and their friends. For instance, a mom might give her child a tickle, as a soothing touch and is acceptable. On the other hand students or children of the same age group can be able to tickle one another and it is acceptable. But it's not appropriate to make a gesture to an adult if you're not in a relationship in a relationship that is not formal.

The act of touching can be a form of abuse

There is usually an undefined line between acceptable contact or physical abuse. If you aren't certain, be cautious about initiating contact unless sure of the meaning for the person being targeted. A person who is pushed or slapped is considered to be a type or physical assault. The act of striking or hitting anyone, and strangling them are all forms of physical abuse.

Touch as an activity

In certain situations, a touch can be a part of game, particularly in the case of teasing. The use of touch as a part of game can only occur when the participants are close to each other and are open to it. For instance, a acquaintance or classmate could cover your eyes by rubbing their palms from behind. The people involved in this kind of tease could touch as an example the blinded person might attempt to touch your head or arms to attempt to guess who is the one they are being teased. In this kind of touching the amount of instruction can be extensive and may be similar to that of lovers.

Chapter 13: Unknown Ingredient In Body Language

"What do you know about your Lord?" "Words," said Hamlet. It seems he should have answered "body communication." In a world where we're obsessive about words, constantly contemplating the next thing we'll say, we pay less focus on our body language. Strange considering that 55% of all communication is transmitted through body language while only 7% of communication involves words.

Consider the reality. 77% of communication is in words. 55% of communication is through body language. It's a shocking fact which will make it clear that if you want to maximize your communication skills, whether professional, social, or any other, you need to utilize body language.

What can you begin now, to make the most of that amazing 55% of communication which is based on body language? There are numerous methods. Let's look at some of those that have become the loved and important.

Conflict Resolution

You might be one of the people who get into disputes often without having an idea of the reason. Certain people create conflicts out of air. One particular person who will be kept anonymous, but who can be used as an excellent illustration is always into arguments. He speaks politely. He doesn't say any wrong thing, but there are always arguments. Why? Because he is nervous in body language. He tucks his arms around his chest. He seldom smiles. He'll even tap on tables or some other object while talking. His words are courteous but his body language is not. His body language shifts from angry to impatient constantly.

If you're among those unfortunate ones that, like our man, is entangled in arguments that seem to come out of nowhere, be sure to look for the negative signs below.

Don't cross your arms in front of your chest.
Don't tap on objects
Do not twiddle with your hair or look at your face.
Smile and make a smile occasionally to let your

employer know that you are content and comfortable

There are many more gestures that we could discuss here, but the goal isn't to provide an exact blueprint for positive body language, but it's to make a thing clear: If you are involved in arguments that which you don't have a rationale to support your argument in your phrases, consider your body expressions. It's likely to be the root of the disagreement. Simple corrective measures here and there can make those arguments an enjoyable discussion.

Body Language and Relationship

Romance is most likely to be the top reason why people study body language. It's a smart move. The fact that five percent of the communication is important in a romantic relationship just like in normal conversation. Making use of positive and persuasive nonverbal signals can do a fantastic job of portraying yourself as a charming and, more importantly, an approachable individual. Here are some tips on how to use nonverbal language to attract attention.

Do not be too fawning however, when you meet

someone new , show them an authentic smile to show that you're glad to meet them. Do this regularly. So when you meet someone you're interested in you'll impress them with your first impression, by saying, "Oh, wow, I really like you. I'm extremely happy that we have met." When spoken in words, this phrase is not much in the sense that if you say it with your body, it's an effective way to communicate and will help start a relationship off on an excellent beginning.

Keep your legs separated by your hips: A few supposed experts will tell men to sit with their legs apart in order to display dominance, which will attract women. The issue, however is that men overdo it. They make a simple posture into a hilariously exaggerated display of their topmost jewels. Simply stand with your legs firmly apart This will display the confidence and the strength.

Lang Gazes: Nervous males and girls may look at someone they like to, and they will look away with a shy smile. Big mistake. It gives the impression that you think that a) you're not strong and the other) you aren't a fan of the person you were looking at (because logic dictates that if you liked admiring them, you'd keep doing it).

The same basic steps are followed; you'll see that small corrective steps like these can will make all the difference.

Let's examine another aspect in which non-verbal communication is vital.
Friendliness
Here are some ideas to help you express your kindness through non-verbal communication while appearing powerful and strong.

Smile enough for people to know that you're content, but don't overdo it.

If you're a person who has a habit of tinkering around with objects or fiddling with yourself, stop. this can make your employer believe that you're bored or bored.

If you are standing and walk around, do not cover your chest, neck stomach or your privates by covering them with obstacles (a barrier could include your arms, purse, an item that you carry, or any other item that could block your path).

Move your feet and belly button toward the person you are talking to. This shows a lot of respect for the person. It can be interpreted as a compliment and will be very well received.

These are just a few from the numerous ways the way that non-verbal communication could have an impact on your daily life. This chapter has shown how you can make use of simple gestures to improve your communication and create stronger relationships. Utilize them and observe the difference you can see in your communication. I'm sure you'll be delighted.

Chapter 14: Body Langue In The Area Of Work

Body language has a myriad of positive outcomes when used correctly when used in the workplace. The benefits include helping inspire colleagues, boost productivity, and help to build stronger connections and relationships, and aid in being more secure and confident. Here are some suggestions about how to take charge of your role and earn the respect you are entitled to.

* Maintain eye contact. This demonstrates confidence, strength and an unquestionable trust factor. Engage your eyes and make sure you're paying attention when you're engaged in conversation. At times, you may look away from conversation. You don't want to look uncomfortable or unnatural but when you make eye contact, move your eyes slowly left to right when you are conversing to ensure that you're paying attention to the conversation.

Try the Power Pose. There have been studies conducted at Harvard as well as Columbia

Business Schools that indicate that putting your body into an "high-power" posture for a few minutes is a great way to increase confidence. The pose is basically that of a strong person In the posture you're in a large amount of space, and your legs and arms are far away from the person, i.e. sitting in a reclining position in which your legs are propped on the desk or with your the chest extended and your hands resting between your hips.

Smile. We can get so caught up in dealing with the stress of our lives that we don't remember to smile. You must put your worries and tension at home and arrive at work as a completely different person, in a sense. A smile indicates that you're an enthusiastic, pleasant welcoming, helpful, and warm person. People will be more inclined to come up to you and interact with them.

Keep their arms folded. We tend to put our arms in a folded position when we aren't sure how other to make of the arms. This isn't a wise choice since it puts you into an aggressive posture and suggests that you're a bit at a distance and trying to shut from the world. By crossing your arms, it suggests being uncomfortable and uneasy in the moment.

* Use your hands to speak. I am sure we've been told not to speak with our hands . We were reminded many occasions how irritating it can be. However studies have proven that using your hands actually aids in arrange your mind, focus your thoughts more clearly, and reduce the use of empty words. Additionally, those who speak using their hands are perceived as friendly, warm and energetic.

SMALL GROUP SITUATIONS

Pay attention to an associate's and subordinate's physique could assist you in deciding whether to proceed. In a one-on-one or small gathering, keeping track of body language can discern a lack of trust or an issue with an existing venture, or perhaps disdainful of the worker. When you are able to assess the body language of a person, you will be able to discern potential problems and locate the solutions.

If the representative isn't confident regarding a particular task further preparation or help is advised. If you feel that there is a problem that was a part of the venture has arisen it's your responsibility to address the problem. The body language of a person can reveal more than what your employees will tell you via their words, allowing you to improve the work environment.

In a relationship of kinship, one's body language could indicate that someone is focused on what the other person is saying. Moving forward in the conversation indicates that the person is in the process of listening to what the other person is saying. Reclining could indicate that he is impartial or believed that he was unrivalled. Moving forward and being close to talk could indicate that someone is trying to convince another person or trying to dominate the conversation. Being able to hear someone's voice without paying attention indicates that you are not in any way by the imagination thinking about them, and are simply waiting for your opportunity to discuss. This gives the person you are talking to impression that you're not thinking about them or what they should say. It's just plain rude!

GATHERINGS or PRESENTATIONS
In introducing yourself or conducting a meeting you can observe the facial expressions of your

guests to determine the manner in which your message was received. Your audience could feel exhausted or disengaged if you observe they keep a deliberate space from looking at each other. They may also play with objects, such as notespads or pens or jot, or exhibit poor posture. Employees or supervisors who feel nervous or are incapable of disproving your point will likely be in opposition of you. They may keep their arms crossed or avoid eye contact. If they appear to be averse to your ideas You can start dialogue to address the issue and come up with solutions with them.

JOB INTERVIEW

In the conference room It's fine to place an untidy display case on the table especially in cases where you'll show its contents However, it's better to place other things on the floor with your. Placing a folder case, or a satchel on your lap can make it appear like you're trying to create an obstacle for your own self, and which alerts Craig.

Do not incline forward that makes you appear to be shutting off, Bowden says. Instead, he recommends to sit straight and show your chest, neck and stomach zone to indicate that you're open.

When you are moving your hands Craig suggests be sure to keep them in the vicinity of the area of work and beneath the collarbone. "Any more than that and you'll appear to be berserk," she says.

Bowden suggests that you keep your hands further back, in what he refers to as the "reality plane" which spreads out 180 degrees around your navel. "Motioning from here demonstrates that you're focused, in control and quiet , and you're in need of help," he says.

It's okay to stand 1 foot from the table to ensure that your signals are clear the man states.

Body language can be the key factor to consider during a potential employee's meet-up. In the event that the person's body language demonstrates that he's at ease with the subject and can pass with certainty, he stands an increased chance of obtaining the job.

Chapter 15: Social Body Language Through Body Contact Touching

Have you ever had the chance to touch someone? When was the last time that you have reached out and touched someone?

The mother's hand is gently touching the cheeks of her baby son; two couples hugging hands; a father putting his hand onto his son's shoulder following an utter defeat in the football match on his Friday night are three instances of touching. It's not just touching that has an impact however, it is the mental thought that is associated with the contact that creates the difference. People touch you by accident or in the intention of doing so. But the impact isn't identical to the three situations mentioned earlier. When someone touches you with a purpose such as the following Biblical account:

"Jesus handed out his hands and touched him" Mathew 8:3; the outcome of Jesus' hand's touch was captivating and life-changing. The man was healed from his illness. Have you recently touched someone to fulfill a particular motive? Have you had someone else in a similar manner touched you? In this article, we will focus on the significance of touching in body language and close this section. Let's begin by stating that words are perceived through the hands.

A word spoken by hand

The gesture of pointing fingers during conversations in America is considered rude and frequently can spark a fight. In other regions of the world the gesture is acceptable. Fingers are pointed at one another frequently to show emotion and to drive home a point. Imagine the official trying to regulate the game of rugby, soccer or basketball through only spoken communication.

In sports, it's all about the action. There is no time for talking time. The instructions and warnings are communicated via body language. This is done by using signals.

Body contact and actions include the eye contact with a direct gaze and speaking loudly and body contact, and touching.

People from different groups in different categories of touch or contact could bring to mind.

Body Language in greetings

What are some significant contact patterns in body language? Farewells and greetings are among the biggest body language differences.

The Japanese bow, while Americans hold hands and shake their heads, hug or maybe even kiss another person.

Heselgrave in his publication "Communicating Christ Culturally" said during her research "The Gururumba of Eastern Highlands of New Guinea initiate their greetings through extending the arm as well as the back with a grip on their buttocks." It's a strange way of greeting, however it is accepted by the group of people. If people in this culture are able to hold the buttocks as part greetings, then you must be able to accept the gesture since it is evident it is a sign of the values of the culture. In street corners in London, (unless of course there are two natives who share an underlying cultural connection have been involved) it may raise eyebrows. If you're not from that tradition, you might not be able to greet your partner with a kiss at the center of a mall.

in the film "Coming to America,"" which stars Eddy Murphy as the prince of the remote and primitive African Zamunda country Zamunda We see an iconic example of body language.

Eddy Murphy is out at the stadium , watching a ball game, while looking at Liza she is that girl of his desires. He departs the venue to answer the calls of nature in the bathroom located nearby. In the bathroom, he is greeted by the local resident from the country of his origin. The man bows and respects him when he greets him.

Eddy is quiet; he does not want to draw attention to his appearance. He thus revealed his identity. He nudges the person to his feet however, the observer is able to discern what the culture norms behind this act of respect to the prince. That's how much power body language has over people who communicate it and also receive it. It doesn't matter where are, if your way of greeting is to rub noses and rubbing your noses, that's the kind of thing you'd do to a other countrymen in street corners in Las Vegas, Papua, New Guinea, or Osaka in Japan. Body language communication goes beyond casual contact, via greetings, and even body contact.

Body-Contact Communication

Your father's age may be visiting you in Kampala or Uganda from the upcountry. You might be able to hold his hand in the streets for peace and safety. In the context of that, there is no problem with this type of physical contact between a person within the United States of America. An explanation or excuse could be required to explain the underlying issue.

In the rural African settlements, it's not common for a man or female to touch in public. The public is not a fan of physical contact. They portray promiscuity.

The same kind of physical contact isn't something that you should pay any attention to in a urban context. A peck on the cheek or a kiss is not uncommon to young people living in third world cities. However, you should not engage in any of these kinds of physical contact in the rural community. You could face the scorn and ire of a few members, or the entire community. an entire.

There is nothing inappropriate to put your arm around your shoulder with a trusted, long-standing acquaintance when you meet one with each other in the street. This is not the case to be done in the West. In the Western hemisphere, customs and practices differ. You could find yourself in the middle of an incident.

Learning taken from Body Language Communication

Three lessons that you can draw from and take away from all non-verbal communication that is discussed in this section as well as throughout the book.

Body Language Recognition

There is a need to appreciate the ways in which body movements and language is utilized and understood by diverse communities.

Communication is a part of many different ways such as clothing and lifestyles, artifacts and symbols of worship.

Wearing neck bands is used by South Ndebele women in Kenya to prove that they are married woman or that the necklaces are worn by Kayan women from Myanmar to keep the possibility of becoming slaves since they are less appealing to enemies, is not considered primitive by a missionary who is compelled to spread Jesus Christ's gospel. Lip gloss , which is worn by modern women may be a sign of attention to detail as they get ready for the day, and also to protect the lips against chapping.

Architectural Structures

It is true that Christianity as well as civilizations came into the Third World from the developed countries. The architects who had western-inspired ideas came along with the Christian missionaries. Finding it difficult to design a an architectural style that is traditional to the church's tradition can be a welcoming and inviting concept, but it's lengthy.

Why not direct your time, talents and resources

toward the ultimate goal -the bigger picture of transformation of the heart that is brought about by the transformative effect by the gospel. In Christianity the primary objective is to preach and instruct. Education, knowledge, and the ability to use it. In the field of medicine, treatment and prevention of illnesses. These are the concerns that must be addressed by both residents and the immigrants, who have a the desire to make life pleasant and prosperous for their families as well as their communities as well as, throughout the process, they're faced with communication issues involving body language.

It's a Way To Lie

Cultural life is ever-changing and is subject to changes. It is not static. The quantity of hours spent exploring different perspectives on body language and methods of interpretation could take away the main reason humans are here on earth, serving and serve.

Chapter 16: Picking Up On Deceptive Body Language Behavioral Clusters

Before we analyze the body language you should be looking for to tell whether someone is trying to fool you, let's look at the reasons the reasons why people attempt to use deceiving. There are many reasons one might want to be deceived, but these two are the most important ones:
* Persuasion
* Avoiding detection

If the the interaction you have with someone else is one of these twoscenarios, and the information below is constantly reflected in the body language, it's likely that they are lying to you.

A person who is deceitful is typically worried about being exposed by the people they are. This worry, most often, reveals:

Anxiety

If they are not highly skilled or psychopathic acting, a deceitful person generally feels stressed. Because of this they send signs of stress. They could be accompanied by rapid, jerky movements, sweating and minor muscle twitches changes in voice tone and so on. Take note that in the case of minor muscle twitches the jaw muscles and the eyes tend to be the most vulnerable. Pay attention to spot deceit.

Control

To avoid being in trouble, you will notice various signs of excessive control. For example, the gestures will appear made up and will usually seem too "cultivated. Be aware of smiles that show the mouth smiles, however the eyes are not smiling in any way. By being honest, it isn't an expression that people use to make up for it If the lips smudge however both eyes don't appear to be smiling, it's fake smiles in which the eyes don't smile.

The person in anxiety may try to keep their body in a position to conceal the signs. For example, they could put their hands into their pockets. Another option is to project their words using either a excessive or limited focus.

Distracted

Someone trying to deceive generally has to think on their feet They must think about their actions than normal. Therefore, they could be distracted, in mid-story, when they are thinking about the next thing they'll say. Be aware of hesitations and sudden awkward pausing.

Anxiety can also trigger the actions of fidgeting, and paying attention to strange locations.

Picking Up on Defensive Body Language
Behavioral Clusters

If someone feels threatened they may adopt defensive postures in order for self-defense. Here are the most basic body language defense postures and responses:

COVERING THE VITAL ORGANS/POINTS OF VULNERABILITY

This involves covering the torso. This is something we've previously discussed. The chin is held to ensure that neck muscles are protected and the groin area is covered with the knees joined or legs crossed. It's an ancient defence mechanism for humans that is in use today, despite the absence of physical danger.

FIGHTING AWAY

The arms could be pushed out in order to keep against the "attacker.' Most likely, though, is the more subtle curved arms pose to deflect injury.

USEING A BARRIER

A physical object can be put between the individual and the addressee in order to serve as a literal and often an metaphorical barrier. It might be an object like a pencil cap , or cabinets. Have you noticed that people relax significantly when they are allowed to sit in an unreversible chair?

Some other examples include cushions that are swaddled against the torso and Teddy bears.

BECOMING SIZY

A way to protect yourself against an attack is to reduce the size of the target. So, for example, people can congregate to create the space in a smaller area, and keep both legs and arms towards.

Rigidity

This is a different primitive reaction. The muscles tighten and become more brittle and able to be able to withstand attacks better. It also freezes the body, which reduces moves that might draw the attention of the predator. This is a standard feature found in the primary food sources of the gazelles as well as rabbits.

Hiding

It's a simple one that a person who feels at risk seeks out the safest space. For instance, you could take a walk along the inner part of the sidewalk or from the street. It is also possible to see someone taking up the most distant corner of a room.

SEEKING EXPANSION

Eyes that move between one eye and another

could indicate that the individual is usually subconsciously looking for a way out.

Pre-empting the "Attack"

Giving-in

The person who is defensive will use the posture of a submissive person, avoid eye contact Keep your head down and possibly crawl if the circumstances allow for it.

FIRST ATTACK

The body language of aggression could be visible when a person adopts the "attack is the most effective defense' attitude. Be aware of an upright body, and quick interjections. Be on the lookout for body language that appears to be 'conflicting. If the upper part of the body is pushed out in a threatening manner, and the legs are crossed or pressing together, the individual just shows aggression due to the fact that he/she is defensive.

Let's now get to read various emotions with the body language you use.

Chapter 17: Don't Forget To Join It!

In its own way, every piece of information you get from studying someone's behavior isn't going to be very helpful. If you focus on one sign, you'll get a limited understanding of the reason why the signal is produced or what it might mean. You should take the time to examine an individual's entire speech to get a better understanding of them and gain more precise understanding of the person they are and the reasons they're expressing themselves in the manner they do.

It may require some time to integrate all the clues until you can reflect on your experiences for a long time after they have ended. This is a great reflection because it gives context to all the aspects I've shared in this book. In the end, you'll be able to examine every signal and then put them within context, to form your own analysis findings. This will happen quickly, so don't stress about spending time investigating every step. When you begin to watch the people around you the speed will increase.

The first step is to use physical cues.
The first thing to look for is physical signs on someone. Before you say hello it is your chance to examine the body of the person and get a sense of their feelings in that particular moment. Take note of their posture, the way they've positioned themselves and the environment they are in, and also what they're doing within the space. If they are performing gestures or movements take note of them and also.

If you are aware of that and/or not have an opinion about the person you are thinking about within your subconscious mind prior to speaking to them. Making a conscious effort to examine their behaviour and their facial expressions and then form an opinion about them is a great method to establish the basis of your study. When you first start to interact with someone be aware of what they behave. It could be that they are the same, but their behavior could change as they're now interacting with a different person. This is a fantastic method to quickly gain insights into the baseline of that person and their personality, and to spot subtleties in their behavior as well as variations from their normal.

Second Step 2: Emotional Cues

It is possible to detect emotional signals through expressions on the face, tone of voice, the words you choose and the general energy of the person you are talking to. Ideally, you should detect the emotional signals of someone before you begin to talk to them , or before you begin the conversation so that you are aware of what you can expect. Being aware of someone's emotional signals will allow you to alter your behavior to be sensitive to their feelings. If you're trying to get something out of them, this provides you with the chance to generate the right emotional response that will get them aligned with you and understanding the words you're saying.

People's emotional cues may rapidly shift; for instance when they see someone, they might be pulled into a different state of mind than the one they had before you arrived or even introducing yourself. Be aware of these shifts can help you comprehend someone's personality and how they are being, as well as the things they're enjoying in the conversation. It is also possible to identify the things they're averse to or avoid due to the negative emotional triggers.

Third Step Third Step: Vocal Cues

When someone begins talking, it is important to be aware of the vocal signals they use. They will let you know how they feel through their voice expressions, words, expressions as well as the extent to which they talk. The ability to listen to a person's voice for clues about how they feel and what they are in need of will confirm the assumptions you've made to this moment. They can also provide an additional layer of context to someone and help you understand their feelings or thoughts. they're thinking.

Vocal cues are the more likely to diverge from the norm and are the easiest to embellish So be cautious when listening to someone's voice. It is possible to hear an energy "behind" the voice that could indicate the emotion they're conveying is not the emotion they're actually experiencing. The hidden emotions could indicate that a person is unsecure or trying to conceal their true emotions, which could suggest that something could be not right.

4th Step Baseline

After a couple of minutes of observation and interaction when suitable, you need to establish your base for that person. From this point you'll quickly analyze the physical, emotional, and verbal signals in order to make an assumption as to what archetype that person has and what they're currently experiencing. Also, you will determine what they are in need of and what they're doing to satisfy the desire.

Your base assumption is not always an accurate one, particularly at first, and it is important to be aware not to act as if it's 100% accurate. Instead, consider it an initial basis to collect data and utilize it to reinforce or challenge your assumptions. When you interact with this person, you will be creating your baseline to ensure that it is more sophisticated and can accommodate greater aspects of their personality like their emotional responses to triggers of different kinds.

Fifth Step Fifth Step: Deviations
Once you've developed an understanding of a person's emotions, you'll be able to start noting any deviations from this. Monitoring deviations should be done only when you have a solid, solid knowledge of their base since this will ensure that you are able to provide a more accurate picture of who they are. When you're sure of their

baseline, you are able to begin to pay attention to deviations.

The signs of deviations will be evident in the person's drastically altered behavior and emotional response to the presence of someone. If someone who is generally calm , suddenly becomes angry or angry, for instance, you can tell they've strayed from their norm. The deviations indicate how the person is feeling, and whether you're trying to provoke a particular response or reaction from them, they can help to determine if you're on the right path or not.

Chapter 18: Speed-Reading People

While you're unlikely to be able to read minds after the book you read but you'll get adept at analysing and decoding people's intentions as well as non-spoken words. You might be thought of as are a mind reader. We've all wanted to be as powerful as Sherlock Homes possesses of speed understanding people's details of the people they were sleeping with the night before. This isn't exactly what you'll find during this book. What you'll get is a method to master this art form. The more you work at it, the more efficient and more precise you'll get. However, it shouldn't be an unending chase. It's not about being able to guess. It's about applying the common sense that is supported by research conducted in the field of science and a deep understanding the human nature. There are five primary research-based aspects you should be aware of in order to read quickly the person standing in the front of you such as context, clusters, the baseline, culture personal bias.

What is the best way to read people? To Read

People

If you wish to be able to read people with greater accuracy There are certain mistakes to avoid, as well as certain factors to keep in mind when analyzing your findings. It is also important to be able to read people with all of you senses not only your eyes or your ears. The five mentioned in greater in greater detail.

* Find a baseline to determine the personality. If you're not sure the way a person behaves under normal, non-threatening circumstances it's just making assumptions based on your research. People behave differently in different ways and it's difficult to read someone's speed and conclude that they're deceiving the person if you're not aware of what they do normally. Some people are simply hyperactive, or they speak in a stutter. That doesn't mean anything. If a body suddenly stop moving, and is as rigid as a stone - it's certainly a red flag. What you must consider to understand the person more clearly is "how does this person typically behave, and is this movement of their body an aspect of their normal behaviour?"

* Culture. It's impossible to effectively identify a person if aren't aware of their culture and the signals they send. Even more, you could miss the signals you're getting. For instance, if you're speaking to someone who is a Latin man, and they're in close proximity to you, it could be perceived as offensive, but for them, it's normal manner of being. It's not a cause for harm. It's the same when it comes to eye movement. In Africa people will stare at you with eyes that are lowered or even not make eye contact. And when you take that to mean fraud, you've killed the relationship. Therefore , it is important to learn to study cultural patterns in the language and their meanings based on the culture you're dealing with. One good inquiry to make when you're not sure is "what's this person's cultural heritage? Does this body's unconscious signal typical in their society?"

Pay attention to your surroundings or context. Don't think that when someone crosses their arms that they are shutting their arms. In the event of a cold room, or the chair they're sitting in lacks any armrests. It's normal for people to be able to fold the arms. In such an environment crossing arms doesn't any information. So what you should be considering when you observe the body posture of a certain person is "should anyone in this situation be acting or posing in this manner?" Be aware of cluster signals. Don't interpret and analyze an individual based on a single message. If you just look for one sign that tells you something and believe that's all it takes to determine the character of the person, you won't succeed in this amazing art. Maybe in films, it might be effective, but in real life, you require more than the appearance of a smile or fidgeting with your hands. Instead, you should be observant of a series of movements that are almost beginning to create an entire story on their own. For instance, someone begins to sweat on their forehead and lips are swollen in a room that is cool and they continue to rub their face, stutter, or struggle to speak as the conversation becomes more in depth. It could be a sign of deceit. What you should consider is "are the majority of this individual's behavior revealing a different truth in relation to what he or she says, or what do they believe that deception is a part of their identity?"

- Be conscious of your own biases. If you do not

increase your awareness of your personal biases it's difficult to discern the right person. The reality is that we're reading people from our own beliefs. So, if you love or dislike someone the way you evaluate the person you are determined by your own perception. If someone praises you, makes feel happy, appears to be like your own, or like the person or attractive, these factors could influence your judgement unconsciously. If you're trying to believe that you're totally impartial then that's likely the biggest bias of all! Nobody expects you to eliminate your biases - you just need to be conscious of your bias.

Learning to Improve Your Speed Reading

It's a strategy that can help you master the art that reads people. It's easy to do and when done properly, it will help you comprehend what someone else is feeling and help you adapt your communication and address the person more efficiently. It's a great method for making sure you have a good rapport and effective communication regardless of who you're communicating with. It can also assist you to quickly identify those who could be risky or harmful to you far before they actually do anything. Like speed reading a book speed reading someone is all about practicing. Where should you begin and what are you listening to and trying to find to speed-read a person?

We've covered a lot of this has been covered before however, let me offer a quick overview of how you could read someone's speed with. The first step is to make a baseline as we've mentioned previously. The baseline will inform you of the habits and the normal behavior of the individual who is at ease. Pay attention to the body's breath, movements, eye movement and the hands and legs to get a full comprehension of how the person is presenting themselves when they talk. Pay attention to their style of speaking and their cadence when they speak on a variety of topics. Once you've established a baseline you can move onto the next step. Start looking for deviations. What you're trying to find is the inconsistencies between the base you've established and the person's movements and expressions. Are there leaky facial expressions? Is the blinking rate increasing? Are they clearing their throat several times suddenly? If you observe inconsistencies, it's best to look further into the issue so that you can begin collecting information to determine your next steps. The next step is to observe the patterns of gestures. You should be able to discern what kind of story the non-verbal signals are conveying. Are they consistent with the narrative the person is telling? In this case, I saw an interview featuring a mother who shot her children . She then took them to the hospital, where they succumbed to the wounds. During the interview one woman trying to convey the depth of her grief through her words was constantly leaking intriguing body movements and facial expressions which actually told a different story. The words she spoke of were ones of sorrow, however her face didn't show any sign of it. Every once in a while, one might spot something that looked like smiling or grin. The descriptions of the horrendous condition of her children did not cause her eyes to water a inch, and she appeared to be in a state of calm (almost like an unmoving rock) when she spoke about how she was grieving for her kids. In this kind of situation it's easy to spot a series of gestures that convey a different story than what the individual is saying using words. This is the kind of thing you have to discover, also. When you find that be cautious, you should take your time since you're likely witnessing deceit moving.

The next step in helping you speed-read an individual is to look at the way they walk, and how they continue to interact with others in the same group or with those around them. What is the person's expression? What happens to body language and posture? It is also important to pay attention for the phrases they select along with their tone and how loud their voice. One of the most important things to look out for, particularly in the event that you're not sure if a person is trying to fool them, could be the series of these four gestures that repeat time and time again. They include hand-to-hand faces, hand touching cross-arms and leaning away. In their own way, none of these signs suggest deceit However, when they are combined they create an captivating story that you ought be aware of.

5 Techniques To Speed Read People

#1. Pay attention to their appearance.
There's lots of non-verbal communication that is passed down through the way people dress. Be aware of their clothes. For instance, a tidy and

professional appearance indicates that the person is a professional. Narcissists spend too much time and effort on their appearance. They may also have a little more muscle (for males) or the cleavage (for females) than I and you would want to. Also, be aware of their facial expressions and whether they're smiling or frowning, for example.

#2. Motions.
Another method to speed read is to watch their general body movements and hand movements. Are there any gestures used to convey a specific message that you must be conscious of? For instance do you see someone who is part of American culture, but moving his head from side opposite (which is interpreted as the negative) and referring to something positive? It could be a red flag is worth keeping an eye on to determine if there is a pattern of them appears.

#3. Be attentive to their language.
This is investigating the way in which the individual is using the language and his voice in order to communicate. Do you hear a clear voice? Does it have a high pitch or is the voice becoming more deep? Is it natural? How is the rhythm? The more you employ this method, the easier it is to

discern the meaning behind statements like "I'm perfectly fine" as well as "it's acceptable." A lot of parents are adept at discerning that they suspect their child is lying, based on the straightforward answer of "I'm being honest," and that's partly because they employ this tactic subconsciously to detect the inconsistent nature of their child's behavior.

#4. Be aware of the mirroring body communication between you. Mirror neurons are inbuilt sensors in our brains which reflect the mood. The brain is equipped to detect our body language and body language of each other and this is a fantastic method to discern what the other person is experiencing. A smile from another person is sure to stimulate the smile muscles in your face, as is a frown. If you're liked by someone then they'll likely have eyebrows that are arched, and you'll see the muscles in their face relaxing and their head tilting slightly. There could be the same thing happening in your body and creates a mutual action between you. If your partner isn't receptive to that behaviour when you start it, they might be sending a signal that they aren't a good fit for you.

#5. Examine immediate or apparent character traits to help discern the type or person that you're working. For instance Does the person seem to be more introverted or extrovert? What kind of relaxed do he / appear? Are they more than a person who feels? What kinds of words do they prefer using? What is the amount of space they want to be able to enjoy between you and them?

Applying these techniques to analyse individuals will require some time of practice, so don't make rash decisions in your judgement and give yourself an extensive sample before declaring yourself an expert in speed reading. Don't forgetthat liars attempt moreoften, and are often insecure with silence. Therefore, the more open and honest your presence is, the simpler to speed and accurately read someone's speed and determine their true motives.

Chapter 19: Body Language In Negotiation

Negotiating successfully involves a lot of things and has nothing to do with doing exactly what you want to say. It's been demonstrated that controlling body language is essential in negotiations, particularly when it's in a professional setting. Learning this crucial skill can help you to make the most earning deal ever. It has nothing to do with the concepts you are taught in classes or at psychology schools. It's a very real process that must be practiced and improved over time. What is most important is the level of mastery you place into it. First and foremost, you must mimic the person's actions as well as body language and general manner of behavior while speaking. By doing this, one can quickly discern the voice and facial expressions of the person speaking, which allows them to establish the trust needed for negotiation. For example, when someone is speaking at the podium with their back to the front and watching the conversation, it can help you connect to the person speaking. The speaker will be aware of your enthusiasm and positive influence your speech has.

In addition, it's the level of interest that is crucial in this scenario, when both the speaker and listener can meet on a shared base of interests. Then, you will be able to connect because a rapport of negotiation was built during the speech. If you are prone to are prone to leaning back and crossing your arms during your speech, the speaker might be wondering whether you're at all interested in the topic they chose or if something is wrong. If this happens, make sure that the conversation began from the negative side and it is possible that you won't be able to win the case. Everyone hates being challenged in any way, so when it comes to negotiations you must challenge your opponent in an approach that is positive.

In addition, the nodding skills of negotiation are a common practice of President Obama's predecessor in the United States, Barrack Obama From his many speeches, you will see this distinctive negotiation skill at work. Obama used this method even in complete disagreement with the delegate He would always smile and maintain eye contact in all situations. The reason for this can be traced back to his stunning victory during the campaign during his speech. If you're able to remember his speech, he's by far the most intelligent and arousing person to date. His style of speaking and how he speaks, and the manner of negotiation he uses in his professional life is unbeatable. That's why he was able to accomplish quite a bit during his time.

Additionally, negotiation skills assist in reducing tension in the masses and create the foundation for a constant alignment towards the goal. Additionally, it helps in building bridges between the whites as well as the blacks of the country. Additionally, the ability to negotiate employed by the highest state official helps the country be able to gain influence through agreements signed by these officials to bring the state up to the same level. How can you convince someone if you are unable to convince yourself? Does it make sense? It is a must-have skill for anyone who wants to be ahead of the curve. It requires patience and an in-depth knowledge of the processes within the system.

Also, one must be attentive to the hands, and how they are employed to communicate an idea. Nervousness and stress are constantly evident in the hands movements. When this happens it is very difficult to conceal the emotions because it is evident all over one's hands. Your hand movements during conversations and how actions are perceived by your hand will tell if the issue is serious or whether you're just having fun with your friends. Furthermore, a mature or wise one will observe the manner in which you use your hands. When your hands are clasped in a tight manner while speaking this can indicate that you're anxious and scared of something. An experienced negotiator will benefit from such situations to gain what they want from you , and even gain the majority of the attention. At this point what it means is that you're vulnerable to attack from any source that could be brought on by any. The process of defending yourself becomes extremely difficult when the signs of vulnerability and incompetence have been noticed. These are indications of weakness and one could easily be a victim of those kinds of mistakes, but doing the weakness in public could ruin the entire relationship. To prevent such tragic incidents, it is important to place hands under the chest and hold the fingers and in front of them to convey confidence when talking. If it's done properly you can gain everything they need from the audience as well as the spectator. What are you looking for to do if not influence of your speech, but the manipulative power that goes along with it, and how to convince people of your own way of thinking. A skilled negotiator knows how to convince people to their own way of thinking or perception, viewpoint and convictions behind their actions. To achieve that influence, it requires an ability that is unquestionable by any person in the society. It is essential to have a lasting impression on the person they are with in order to be admired by the the general public. A person with influence is always aware of how to use hand when speaking or communicating with other people in public.

The way you place your feet during negotiations speak for the negotiation itself. It could either help you sell yourself out or cause you to sink into the pit. While it isn't anything to be concerned with the negotiation it is easy to see the situation from your feet, especially if they are securely planted in the ground or is shrinking over the other in a sitting or standing position. It is possible to discern in the right way when your foot is disoriented to indicate that you're anxious or uncomfortable with the situation. You can tell if you're lying or being honest by watching your feet.

In the same way, non-verbal communication is a key element in negotiations. The results of these behaviors reflect openness and trust, as well as honesty that support the positive behaviour that is seen in the majority of the top performers. If they use the appropriate negotiation skills, they will come to a mutually satisfactory agreement at the conclusion of the day. What people do reflect their actual attitude, their mindset and how they view things, and how they conduct themselves in every situation. If one can determine their true attitudes and motives, you can gain a complete understanding of their lifestyle and make negotiation simple.

It is advisable to know more about the person you're going to talk to prior to making any moves. Knowing their beliefs, culture and their perceptions they have of the subject can help to improve the possibility of a successful negotiation. You must show up on time the day they have to discuss any topic. It will help in getting the discussion off to begin on the right track and also shows that you are a time-setter and appreciate everything that's needed to get the right time, without running around trying to get around with a different approach. What do

www.ingramcontent.com/pod-product-compliance
Lightning Source LLC
Chambersburg PA
CBHW050401120526
44590CB00015B/1774